COMPARATIVE
FUNCTIONALISM

COMPARATIVE FUNCTIONALISM

An Essay in Anthropological Theory

———

WALTER GOLDSCHMIDT

UNIVERSITY OF CALIFORNIA PRESS

BERKELEY AND LOS ANGELES   1966

University of California Press
Berkeley and Los Angeles
California
Cambridge University Press
London, England
© 1966, by The Regents of the University of California
Library of Congress Catalog Card Number: 66-14412

To that ambiance
created by the community of scholars at
THE CENTER FOR ADVANCED STUDY
IN THE BEHAVIORAL SCIENCES
under the skillful guidance of
DR. RALPH W. TYLER AND HIS STAFF
this essay is gratefully dedicated

PREFACE

The anarchic state of anthropological inquiry is troubling an increasing number of its practitioners. Anthropology holds a monopoly on a body of data which is of prime importance to the understanding of every discipline treating with the nature of man and the character of his behavior. It has a responsibility therefore to the behavioral sciences as a whole, which it cannot neglect but which, in fact, it has not fulfilled.

Only by the examination of human behavior in the wide diversity of discrete historic developments and various cultural settings can we hope to learn what man is like, what his potentialities are, what limitations he is subject to, what he is. It is a basic assumption of this essay that investigation into human nature is legitimate. But because it is part of human nature to live in communities according to learned patterns of behavior, we can arrive at an understanding of that nature only by examining the empirical evidence of ongoing human activity. Only the cross-cultural approach provides that triangulation necessary for a measurement of man.

Anthropological inquiry has taught us to appreciate the phenomenon of culture. It has appropriately drawn us away from the former naïve biological thinking and has led us to the realization that each person is shaped by his culture and each culture is shaped by its own past. It was an important lesson to have learned, but we have learned it all too well, taught it all too insistently. The excesses of current anthropological doctrine lead us to the assumption that man is a perfectly plastic thing and that cultures can take any form.* This, to say the least, is a questionable position, but it is a position that is all too rarely questioned.

The response to this anthropological overstatement is not to return to biological thinking, not to explain human diversity in terms of genetic composition nor human behavior in terms of biological responses— though, I suspect, there is a danger that such an intellectual movement will take place. Rather, it is to recognize the biological in man, the fact that each culture is only to be seen as a patterned response to the character of human needs and each society is shaped by the insistent demands that life exerts on the living. The ethologist can establish behavioral patterns of a species by studying any sample he may find; the anthropologist can obtain an ethological

* As, for instance: "Man is accepted [by social anthropologists] as a plastic organism, whose actions and temperament are moulded by the society and culture into which he is born" (Gluckman 1965:30).

understanding of man only by cutting through the
cultural determinants, and this he can do only by
examining the consistencies which underlie the vari-
ant manifest patterns of behavior. It is not reasonable
to doubt that such consistencies exist.

Anthropology has had a great impact on the moral
philosophy of our time, an impact out of all proportion to the numerical and fiscal strength of the
discipline. It has moved us away from biological
thinking and toward an appreciation of the force of
culture; it has made us aware of our own customs and
beliefs as one of the many and apparently arbitrary
modes of thought. In doing this it has promoted a
cultural relativism, and this in turn has placed anthropology itself in the mainstream of an old scientific
tradition. For as astronomy moved the earth away
from the center of the universe and biology moved
man out of his unique position in the living world, so,
too, anthropology has removed Western man from
the pinnacle and quintessence of human perfectibility
and placed him with the Australian aborigine and the
Hottentot as one of so many diverse cultural beings.*

* Franz Boas, more than any other scholar, was responsible for this ideological shift, which now is taken for
granted not only by all anthropologists but by most in-
tellectuals in the West. Consider this paragraph from
Boas:
"It might seem that the low value given to life in primitive society and the cruelty of primitive man are indica-
tions of a low ethical standard. It is quite possible to show
an advance in ethical *behavior* when we compare primitive
society with our own. Westermarck and Hobhouse have

This has been a beneficial, a necessary intellectual achievement, and while anthropology did not do it unaided, it has had a major role in this intellectual movement.

But however much we may take pride in this influence, however much it was necessary to gain a relativistic view of culture and of our own patterns of behavior, we cannot escape the fact that this is essentially a negative achievement. The positive accomplishment of a theory of man has not been developed, and there seems to be little evidence on the horizon that it is developing as we worry over the kinship system of obscure tribes or the minutiae of native taxonomies. This is not to decry the importance of detailed analysis, it is not a plea to study global problems or large-scale societies; rather it is an urgent request to concern ourselves with the theoretical relevance of what we are doing. If anthropology has a monopoly on a body of data which is essential to the understanding of the human animal, the discipline has a moral obligation to make the best use of that heritage—the more so in that it is a rapidly dwindling resource.

---

examined these data in great detail and have given us an elaborate history of the evolution of moral ideas. Their descriptions are quite true, but I do not believe that they represent a growth of moral *ideas*, but rather reflect the same moral ideas as manifested in different types of society and taking on forms varying according to the extent of knowledge of the people" (Boas 1962:220–221).

PREFACE

This essay is but an effort to suggest a mode of
inquiry, a manner of recognizing the theoretical
relevance of the material of anthropology for the
significant problems in the behavioral sciences. I am
aware that it is programmatic rather than conclusive,
as I am aware of many of its other limitations. I
believe that, however awkwardly, it nevertheless
points the way to a mode of inquiry and I hope, at
least, that it will provoke discussions of the central
issues of the science of man.

Comparative functionalism is a notion that has its
roots in earlier work, but which grew under the
special intellectual climate provided by the Center for
Advanced Study in the Behavioral Sciences, where
this volume was written. I would not want to impli-
cate other Fellows who shared my year at the Center
in anything I have said here, yet I must record that
the stimulation of their cumulative presence inspired
the effort. I am particularly indebted to those who
read one or another draft of the paper and gave me
the benefit of their advice, particularly G. P. Baerends, Max Black, Erik Erikson, Luciano Gallino,
Fred Greenstein, John Seeley, and Robert Waller-
stein. I also express my thanks to my colleagues
Robert Edgerton and Francis Conant for their useful
and critical comments, and to Mrs. Donna Nelson,
who assisted me in numerous intellectual and biblio-
graphical details. Mrs. Irene Bickenback and Mary W.

Schaeffer, who deciphered difficult manuscript copy, deserve special thanks. Miriam Gallaher's sharp and beneficent editorial eye has much improved the writing. August Frugé and Joel F. Walters of the University of California Press have also been most helpful. My debt is great to the entire staff of the Center, from the Director to the cooks; those of us who have had the privilege of participation know how much their kindness and consideration have contributed to our work.

W. G.

Woodside, California
May, 1965

CONTENTS

I

INTRODUCTION

This is a call for a new theoretical approach in social anthropology. Specifically, I propose that the time has come to go beyond the insightful structural analyses of individual social systems and the comparison of institutions, and turn to the comparative analyses of *social functions*. Such a notion has been implicit in functional theory for a long time; its advent has had to await a more sophisticated cross-cultural sociology: in my opinon it is time to initiate such a program.*

Simple as the basic statement is, it raises complexities of a high order; it involves a new and often, even to the anthropologist, difficult view of cultural phenomena. In this essay I want to broach some of these problems. This presentation will demonstrate the

* Julian Huxley suggested ten years ago that anthropological studies should develop a comparative physiology (Huxley 1955:11), a sentiment echoed by Gabriel Almond (1960:13).

impasse of present structural-functional research, then discuss the theoretical problem in a comparative functional approach and, finally, demonstrate the usefulness of this approach with some simple examples.

The ultimate aim of anthropology is the scientific understanding of human social behavior and a systematic understanding of the distribution in time and space of its manifestations. The endeavor to achieve this aim has resulted in many diverse schools of ethnology, and while one may view with dismay both the limited achievements and internal disagreements, one must recognize that the general level of sophistication has risen remarkably considering the short span and limited facilities of our discipline. Among the achievements which anthropologists may take pride in are (1) the general recognition of the phenomenon of culture and the implication of cultural sets for the manifest attributes of humans in their natural habitat; (2) the recognition that man-in-society places certain demands upon the situation in which humans operate so as to affect the character that culture may or must take under given circumstances; and (3) that there is an interrelationship (as yet poorly explored) between the manifestations of social life and the psychological character of the human animal.

Of these three areas of critical intellectual development the focus here will be on the second, but the other two cannot be entirely avoided. It has been popular in certain circles to discount the "cultural" explanation, and particularly to point to the inadequacy of post-Boasian anthropological theory. Yet the contribution of Boas was precisely to insert this cultural dimension into social philosophy. Though Boasian theory is inadequate and weak in terms of present-day understandings—chiefly for some of its negative crotchets—it put the ultimate lie to racialist thinking and has had a tremendous impact on the generic conception of man and his behavior.

The relationship of anthropology to psychological considerations is of a different order. An unfortunate aspect of the Comptean legacy of "levels" in science has been the fear of reductionism. The natural territorialism of scholarly disciplines is aggravated by the assumption that some subjects lie deeper, and the fear of "reducing" phenomena of one level to those of another. This has resulted in a kind of phobia in which the student of social science hesitates to make *any* assumptions (or, rather, any *explicit* assumptions) about the nature of man; yet it can easily be shown that latent assumptions about mankind are hidden in the most hard-headed social theorists, even though they refuse to admit they have any notions or preconceptions about man's biological requirements or psychic characteristics.

One of the most fruitful lines of inquiry in twentieth-century anthropology is that of comparative sociology. The essence of this approach (it lacks the preciseness to call it a method) is the awareness (1) that patterns of social behavior have social causes, (2) that there is an interrelation among various institutional patterns within a community, and (3) that these institutions perform functions in the maintenance of the social order. For instance, Durkheim in his *Suicide* was clearly concerned with the first of these, Weber in his *Protestant Ethic* with the second, and Radcliffe-Brown, in explaining the function of certain rites of passage among the Andamanese, was concerned with the third. This tradition has produced a great body of literature, has developed a whole new way of looking at human behavior, and above all has validated sociological analysis as essential to an understanding of the human condition. Such results are no mean accomplishment, even though, as their critics have pointed out, the social anthropologists have not established any laws of social behavior, as they had boldly set out to do, although that should, in my opinion, be the continuing ambition of all scientific endeavor.

The essence of comparative sociology * is, and

---

* I use the phrase "comparative sociology" to refer here to a type of analytic treatment of social systems, where the focus is on comparison; this is normally the work of anthropologists—not sociologists in the professional sense. The confusion between the professional association and the functional operation is unfortunate but unavoidable, but let it be understood that in this essay, when I refer

must remain, the comparison of social behavior as it manifests itself in the various communities that come under anthropological scrutiny. Yet a good deal of social anthropological work involves the close examination of the internal relationships of institutions within a single social system, analyses which are insightful in their perception and have added to our feeling about the character of the social order.

The central theme of this essay may be summarized as follows: Existing approaches, though they have deepened our scholarly understanding of the human scene, do not admit of scientific diagnosis of the character of man-in-society; such a diagnosis can be developed only in terms of a model; the essence of this model lies in a recognition of the universality of functions to which institutions are a response rather than (as has been characteristic) a primary concern with institutions as such. Such a model of social functions must be seen as operating within a context which includes the nature of man as a being, the character of the environment in which he operates, and the cultural appurtenances he is heir to; and the test of functional assumptions takes cognizance of the circumstances in which the society is operative and the consequences that can be shown to derive from

---

to sociologists or sociological analyses, I refer to those sociologically oriented anthropologists concerned with the structuring of interpersonal relationships, and their works, unless the context clearly indicates otherwise.

the absence of functional performance. I believe that anthropology has come to an impasse, and that the impasse requires a bold new approach to the data at hand, and that a comparative functional approach is a way out of our dilemma.

II

THE MALINOWSKIAN DILEMMA

In this chapter I want to show why I believe that the goal of social anthropology cannot be achieved by existing methods, if the scientific understanding of social phenomena is accepted as the proper goal. Essentially, there are two existing approaches in social anthropology: (1) the detailed internal analysis of individual cultures which generally endeavors to establish interrelationships between diverse sets of institutions—best exemplified by the investigations of Malinowski and generally called functional studies; and (2) the comparison of institutions or structural features among a group of societies (either delimited or worldwide) showing the distribution and covariation of such features. I intend in the following sections to explore each of these in some detail to indicate why neither of them can lead to a satisfactory solution of the subject of anthropological inquiry.

The essence of the problem lies in what I call the

7

Malinowskian dilemma. Malinowski was most insistent that every culture be understood in its own terms;
that every institution be seen as a product of the
culture within which it developed. It follows from
this that a cross-cultural comparison of institutions is
essentially a false enterprise, for we are comparing
incomparables. Yet the internal mode of analysis can
never give us a basis for true generalization and offers
no means of extrapolation beyond the local time and
place. Indeed, it leaves us clearly in the hands of the
Boasians, to whom each culture is merely a product
of its own history. If we are to avoid the stricture that
anthropology must either be history or nothing, we
must find a way out of this dilemma.

Functional Studies

The Malinowskian internal analysis of culture has
demonstrated the interrelated character of cultural
components and has shown that it is possible to
"explain" existing elements in terms of presumed
functions. When well done by an honest and perceptive student it can lead to real insights. But the
extrapolation of these insights to other cultures,
which Malinowski endeavored to do inferentially in
the titles of his more important works—e.g., *The
Father in Primitive Psychology, The Sexual Life of*

Savages—is by the very nature of the enterprise quite impossible.

The intellectual limitations of the functional approach have been subjected to a searching critique by Carl G. Hempel (1959:271) and to extensive analysis by Ernest Nagel (1961) and, more recently, in the symposium prepared by Martindale (1965), particularly the contribution by Jarvie (1965). Hempel shows that so long as the student "explains" facts internally, either (1) he cannot demonstrate that his presumed causes are anything more than circumstances, or (2) they are tautological. This can readily be exemplified. Let us examine some sections of Evans-Pritchard's study of Nuer marital regulations (Evans-Pritchard 1951). As all students of social anthropology must know, the Nuer have a segmentary lineage structure, a system through which, according to Evans-Pritchard, both the local autonomy and Nuer-wide political action are operative. Inasmuch as this mode of social articulation is built upon the idiom of kinship, it follows that kin rules and hence marital regulations are of greatest import to Nuer social life. In the volume at hand, Evans-Pritchard develops (among other things) the rules and regulations governing marriage, and, as the Nuer are rather free in their extra-marital sexual activity, this involves as well the rules of incest regarding adultery and fornication. We need not review these complications in detail, but may focus on certain conclusions.

In view of the importance attached to children by Nuer in determining what is incest, or the degree of it, it may readily be understood *why* sexual relations with the wives of half-brothers, paternal uncles, and patrilineal cousins of every degree are regarded as being either incestuous peccadillos or not incestuous at all. The wife of a 'bull' is, in a general social sense, the wife of all the 'bulls', of the paternal kin, and of the lineage. She is 'our wife' and 'the wife of our cattle'. Likewise her children are the children of the lineage, of the agnatic group, and of its cattle. *Hence* sexual relations with wives of these agnates, if not approved, are condoned, for they are the wives of all. *Hence*, also, whereas relations with, for example, the wife of the maternal uncle means relations with the *cek nara*, the maternal uncle's child, relations with the wife of the father's brother's son are with '*cekdan*', 'our wife', and the mother of '*gatdan*', 'our child'. The presence of a child does not alter the status of the persons concerned in the second case as it does in the first, for the wife is the wife of the lineage and the child is the child of the adulterer. When a man dies, *therefore*, there is no question of the widow being remarried to one of his brothers, for the brothers already count as her husbands. The dead man's lineage have a right to inherit his wife *because* she is their wife, the wife of their cattle.

I think that we should try to interpret in much the same way the feeling that it is wrong for two kinsmen to court the same girl, unless they are members of the same lineage. Paternal kin can share the same girl *because* they have a lineage identity, whereas the courting of the same girl by, for example, a man and his maternal aunt's son *makes for* confusion within the kinship system. The position of the uterine brother is peculiar *because* full brothers are not just 'bulls' to one another, members of the same lineage. They are maternal kinsmen as well as paternal kinsmen, and in their case sexual relations with each other's sweethearts seem to the Nuer to involve in some way the mother, an idea which is repugnant to them (Evans-Pritchard 1951:45–46; I have emphasized the relevant causational terms).

Now this explanation fits the Nuer facts; that is, the Nuer attitudes are as stated (or so we may assume), and the Nuer do treat wives of agnates as accessible, they do rationalize a tabu against a person of certain kin on the basis that they are related through the next descending generation. This latter, being the truly unique element in the Nuer situation, is what Evans-Pritchard ought to be explaining instead of using it as an explanatory device for other, more usual, aspects of behavior.

But is this an explanation at all? It happens that my own most recent field work has been with a pastoral people who share a good deal of the cultural characteristics of the Nuer; namely, the Sebei, a "Nilo-Hamitic" people of Uganda, also cattle-keepers. Many of their regulations are identical to those of the Nuer, as, for example, the tabu against marriages (or sexual access) of a man with the daughter of his agemate. Yet it is precisely against the Sebei rules for a man to have adulterous relations with the wife of any man he calls brother, particularly his own brothers, as well as with any wife of his father (whether or not his own mother), while no such regulation applies to the wives of his mother's kindred. (Of course, such relations are at any rate adulterous and therefore not approved, but the Sebei, like the Nuer, are not meticulous regarding marital fidelity.) In short, though in many ways similar in their social organization and marital regulations, in this matter they are precisely the reverse of the Nuer. The Sebei explain that a man may not have intercourse with his close agnates' wives because these are women whom he might inherit and therefore to have intercourse with them would be tantamount to the expression of a death wish. But this is the *Sebei* explanation; it is not a functional one. It relates to the strong sibling rivalry endemic among the Sebei, though I confess that I do not see why Sebei brothers should be more in conflict than Nuer brothers, and I cannot, at this time, account for the Nuer permissibility as against Sebei restriction on sexual intercourse between a man with his brother's wife.

Evans-Pritchard himself has some discomfort in this "explanation"; the subsequent paragraph reads:

These interpretations may be unacceptable to the reader. If so, he can disregard them without rejecting the main conclusion from which they are inferred. It is clear that the marriage prohibitions indicate kinship status and are one of the most effective means of doing this and thereby maintaining the kinship system, which is based on the distinctions between the various categories of relationships. They prevent confusion between one relationship and another and the contradictions such confusion would cause between the patterns of behaviour in which the relationships are expressed. This conclusion is contained in the statements . . . of Nuer themselves, who see that it is undesirable to obliterate or obscure the boundaries between kinship categories. Were marriage with the wife's sister permitted, to the child of it the mother's sister would also be the father's wife; and were a man to marry the daughter of an age-mate, his age-mate would also be his father-in-law (Evans-Pritchard 1951:46).

But this explanation is either sheer tautology or not true. As a matter of fact, Evans-Pritchard's preceding chapter developed in detail the machination, the legal fiction, and the complicated maneuvering to establish kin connections, where needed, when they do not naturally exist. That is, on the one hand the Nuer override certain complexities in order to assert kinship; they create complexities through their ideology which they (and Evans-Pritchard) use to explain their regulations. The inadequacy of this kind of functional analysis was elegantly expressed in the critique of Godfrey Leinhard when he asked: "Are we doing much more than giving our own version of the myths by which these peoples themselves validate their [social] order?" (Leinhardt 1964:7).*

* Raymond Firth had earlier made a similar point when, in a review of Fortes' *The Web of Kinship among the Tallensi*, he wrote that "native formulations themselves

But we may note in passing that Leinhardt himself does not get out of the charmed circle of "functional" explanation when he endeavors to show that among a group $(N = 4)$ of closely related Nilotic tribes the emergence of political authority is a function of matri-oriented kin involvements in these patrilineal social systems. "If [he writes] I am looking for tiniest germs of political leadership among any people with balanced segmentary lineage systems, I should be inclined to look for it where most emphasis seemed to be placed by sons on the link with the mother's lineage" (Leinhardt 1964:10).

If I follow his reasoning correctly at this point, wives in polygynous households are naturally jealous for their own sons. However: "Whilst this situation remains in the household, that is, while the unity, accompanied of course by structural opposition of the various sons of a single father, is as strong as the competitive principles represented by their different mothers, a simple balance between fission and fusion is preserved as with the Nuer. But where it is possible for a son to turn to his mother's agnates for help against his father's, the competition present in the relations between co-wives is developed in group relations, and there, I think, we see the beginning of specialization of political role" (Leinhardt 1964:8).

---

have often played a significant role in providing some of the anthropologist's mental furniture" (Firth 1951:157).

But who decides what causes which? Might one not equally have said, where political institutions exist, the social importance of the corporate kin groups is reduced by the very fact of an external decision-making institution, thereby making dual alliance more feasible? Or more useful?

This exercise can be shown to apply to all of these insightful internal explanations, as Hempel demonstrated. But we must not deprecate the functional study of individual societies; they have enriched our understanding of the social complexities, sensitized us for new involvements, and given meaning to the idea of sociological explanation of social phenomena. As developed, they are not amenable to proof (or to disproof; my expectation implicit in the query of the preceding paragraph can neither be sustained nor controverted by Leinhardt's material). What is important, though, is that however many such functional studies we obtain, and however increasingly intricate, subtle, and clever they become, they cannot of themselves demonstrate anything more than the infinite complexity of the subject of anthropological inquiry.

The Comparison of Institutions

If the generalizations evoked by the ever-closer analyses of individual social systems are to be either validated as true causal statements or established as significant generalizations about human social behavior, they will have to be examined cross-culturally. As an examination of Oscar Lewis' (1955) essay, "Comparisons in Cultural Anthropology," indicates, these generally leave much to be desired. Occasionally a sharp comparison, such as that of Nadel (1952) on African witchcraft, satisfactorily establishes significant covariation. More often, however, the "comparative" institutional studies are actually nothing more than symposia—containing relatively insightful individual essays with more-or-less cogent introductions endeavoring to point out some common ground.* Such volumes offer us items side by side, and we can make such comparisons as strike our fancy (if the data for each group are available), but they are not comparative studies even in the loosest scientific sense of that term.

The usual pattern among social anthropolgists of engaging in cross-cultural inquiry is to focus upon an institution, usually one of major proportions—the family, marriage, the state—but occasionally a lesser one such as cross-cousin marriage, joking relationship, and the like. The end result is usually either an

---

* As, for example, *African Systems of Kinship and Marriage* (Radcliffe-Brown and Forde, eds. 1950), *African Political Systems* (Fortes and Evans-Pritchard, eds. 1940), *African Worlds* (Forde, ed. 1954), and, more recently, *Matrilineal Kinship* (Schneider and Gough, eds. 1962) and *Markets in Africa* (Bohannan and Dalton, eds. 1962).

elaboration of taxonomies or the proliferation of terminological disputes (or both). The latter are never resolved, while the former often become so complex that each possible sub-subtype contains but a single case. This, it seems to me, has happened with respect to the discussion of residence rules.

I should like to examine a recent controversy in this arena of discourse to show the kind of fallacies that a sophisticated use of such a procedure leads to. I have chosen as an example a long-standing terminological controversy; namely, that regarding the definition of marriage. From a commonsense point of view, marriage appears to be a simple enough institution and one readily defined, but if one knows the variety of rights, privileges, secondary involvements, and circumstantial factors, one finds that this is not the case.

I shall take as my point of departure a paper by Dr. E. Kathleen Gough (1959), not out of criticism of her work, but precisely because of the very thoroughness and thoughtfulness of Dr. Gough's presentation. Dr. Gough has sought a minimal definition of marriage, which she feels will satisfactorily include all cases where marriage exists, and by means of which we can explore the institution cross-culturally. She is responding to an earlier article by E. R. Leach (1955) in which he reexamines the concept of marriage in the light of analyses of polyandry made by H. Th. Fischer and H.R.H. Prince Peter of Greece and Denmark, as well as some earlier presentations by Gough.*

The significant element of Professor Leach's contribution is that definitions of marriage are inadequate, that marriage involves an expandable number of specific social actions, of which Leach himself lists no fewer than ten, that in no society does the institution which we generally call marriage necessarily include all these elements, nor are any of them universally found in marriage institutions. Needless to say, he is working away from the standard definition as found in *Notes and Queries*.† He says that "if we agree that the Nayar practice polyandrous marriage then we are using the term marriage in a sense different from that employed by Fischer and by *Notes and Queries*." Leach demonstrates mounting impatience with this approach, for though his discussion of marriage is temperate in tone and partial in realization, his later essay, "Rethinking Anthropology," ‡ is both immoderate in tone and far more fully

---

* Appropriate citations of these earlier elements in the discussion will be found in Leach (1955). As they will not enter directly into our discussion, these citations may here be omitted.

† As cited by Leach: "Marriage is a union between a man and a woman such that children born to the woman are legitimate offspring of both partners" (Royal Anthropological Institute 1951).

‡ The title essay of *Rethinking Anthropology* (Leach 1961).

realized in intellectual reconstruction. Castigating in the later essay the "butterfly collecting" (i.e., the natural history phase of our discipline), he calls for an algebraic (more specifically a topologic) mode of analysis. This, I believe, is in the spirit of the call for a comparative functional approach, but is not its substance.

Dr. Gough's paper stands in defense of the essence of the *Notes and Queries* definition, though in the process she alters some of its substance. More specifically she demonstrates with clarity and vigor that the Nayars (who inevitably serve as one of those marginal test cases) in fact do involve both (1) a relationship between persons and (2) a legitimization of the offspring.

We need a few essential facts of Nayar social life in order to proceed with our problem, and I take these from Gough. The Nayar live in linked matrilineages, with a variety of reciprocal obligations among them. Each prepubescent girl undergoes a kind of ceremonial wedding (*tali*-rite) with a man drawn from another lineage in the linkage, after which he might, but need not (and usually does not), have sexual contact with her. This ceremony was necessary to the legitimization not only of her future children, but also of her own status as an adult in the community; still, it did not confer either rights or privileges by one party over the other, sexual or economic. The woman remained free, with certain social and kin restrictions, to have men visit with her. A woman normally had several such liaisons: liaisons that were essentially sexual and noneconomic and nonsocial (i.e., in the sense of not creating a sodality of any kind). However, whenever she became pregnant, one (or more) of her sexual partners was expected to give recognition of his (social) paternity by the payment of the midwife fees, an act absolutely essential to the social validation both of the child and of the woman in her role as child's mother (but an insignificant economic contribution). That is, there were two ritual acts normally involving two (or more) different men, one providing that the woman should have a "husband," or more explicitly that she was legally endowed with the right to procreate, while the other provided the child with a ritual father, or rather that the child obtain and his mother retain appropriate status in the community. Gough summarizes her conclusions that this constitutes marriage as follows:

I regard Nayar unions as a form of marriage for two reasons. One is that although plural unions were customary, mating was not promiscuous. Sexual relations were forbidden between members of the same lineage on pain of death. It was also forbidden for two men of the same property-group wittingly to have relations with one woman, or for two women of the same property-group to have relations with one man. (This rule of course automatically excluded relations between a man and his biological daughter.) Further, relations were absolutely prohibited between a Nayar woman and a man of lower sub-caste or caste. These prohibitions are directly connected with my second and more important reason for regarding these unions as marriage, namely, that the concept of legally established paternity *was* of fundamental significance in establishing a child as a member of his lineage and caste.

Granted that Nayar unions constituted a form of marriage, we must, I think, classify them as a clear case of group-marriage.

In order to bring her situation into conformity with a generalized definition, Gough must, as I have already indicated, redefine marriage, which she does as follows: "Marriage is a relationship between a woman and one or more other persons, which provides that a child born to the woman under circumstances not prohibited by the rules of the relationship, is accorded full birth-status rights common to normal members of his society or social stratum." There follows upon this a page or so of exegesis and justification. Among those marginal cases which are to be kept in mind during such a discussion is the Nuer practice of "marriage" between two women, where the ritual provides for having legitimate offspring, as Evans-Pritchard (1951 *passim*) has pointed out. Dr. Gough does not claim, within this redefinition, either (1) that all societies or all ethnic entities necessarily must have an institution of marriage, or (2) that marriage is the only way in which children may be legitimized.

Though this definition so manipulates verbal symbols as to account for the marginal cases which have entered into the controversy, it is still useful to see whether Gough's definition actually is satisfactory. Are there ritual acts which we intuitively call marriage that do not provide for legitimization of children (or potential children)? Are not the "marriages" among male homosexuals (Hooker, 1965; also personal communication) in our society such a case, at least as clearly as the orthosexual "marriages" of the Nuer? Must they be relegated to some other category because they are found in a subculture, or a deviant group, or simply because they are a part of our culture as against some exotic one? *

Gough has, in fact, stripped the term marriage to a

* Of course, both homosexual marriages and Nuer orthosexual marriages are not the characteristic pattern of the respective whole cultures. They demonstrate interestingly the principle of the Malinowskian *cultural* definition, for in each case they are marriages in the analogic sense to counterpart institutions of their own culture. That is, Nuer orthosexual marriages specifically serve the function of creating a relationship analogic to that of a father to provide for a proper social identification for the child. Homosexual marriages provide institutional support for sexual fidelity and establish rights and obligations between the partners comparable to those of heterosexual marriages in our society. Thus, each is analogic, but the central element in the analogy is a different social function. Nuer orthosexual marriages thus bear no relation whatsoever to Western homosexual marriages; each is fully incomprehensible to the other group.

single criterion, though unwittingly so; she creates the equation: *marriage equals provision of birth-status rights to children.* She does this by eliminating all others except the wide open: *a relationship between a woman and other person*(s), which is a nondiscriminating criterion, since as stated it can include all possible human social relationships, except where no women are involved, which is a redundancy to the biological fact that it is woman's lot to bear the child and give it birth.

Even when Gough has successfully stripped the term of all its commonsense meaning, she has not satisfied the requirements of a cross-cultural definition of marriage. Her failure is not lack of knowledge or insight; it stems from the fact that she is endeavoring to do the impossible. We will return to the Nayars' case in a later section.

Let us next examine Leach's procedure, for Gough rightly suggests that Leach has in effect said: "Let us abandon any true definition." Instead he offers a syndrome of classes of rights which "marriage" may entail, all of which are widely recurrent and associated with the union of man and woman, but no one of which is universally found in such association.

"The point I would make [Leach writes] is that in no single society can marriage serve to establish all these types of rights simultaneously; nor is there any one of these rights which is invariably established by marriage in every known society." That is, no matter how many criteria are brought to bear, none will be expressed in each case available in the literature.

Leach, in short, suggests that we split the institution marriage into its component elements and preserve the commonsense meaning of the word. He does not really say why one should do this nor what the units are. As he calls them "sub-types of institutions," and "classes of rights," and treats them each as rights or obligations, we are led to believe they are structural entities rather than functions.

In endeavoring to break the institution of marriage into separate units Leach is making a start at functional analysis, but he has not caught the implications of his own act. For one thing, he treats the units as structures rather than as functions; for another, he has not indicated what problems this would solve or what research program it would engender; and, finally, he has not indicated a rationale for selecting the elements he chose to list. We do not see, therefore, how such listing leads us into a useful system of comparative analysis regarding the character of marriage; it could, at best, lead us to further fruitless taxonomies—or so it would appear from Leach's essay alone.

Leach is in direct opposition to Gough, who says: "I would argue that for cross-cultural purposes we need a single, parsimonious definition, simply in order to isolate the phenomenon we wish to study." And in her concluding paragraphs: "My definition should therefore enable us to isolate marriage as a cross-cultural phenomenon, and from there to proceed to the more exciting task: that of investigating the differential circumstances under which marriage becomes invested with various other kinds of rights and obligations."

I am concerned with the epistemological implications of such a statement. It implies that there is something that may be called *marriageness* existing out there in the world, some substance of which most, if not all, societies partake. If we sometimes worry about the reification of *cultural* concepts, if we are troubled (as I think we must be) as to whether culture lies in the individual or in the group, then we must certainly be concerned with the metaphysical position of such a concept which is beyond the nowhere. When a virologist isolates a culture strain or a pharmacologist finds a particular chemical substance in different plants, he is dealing with something that has concrete and reproducible characteristics, manifestly and verifiably the same, that is mutually interchangeable with substances found elsewhere. We borrow the idiom as a manner of speaking, but we find ourselves enslaved by its semantic implication. Marriage (or family, clan and each of the other concepts of social structure) does not exist as something which is there if only we could put it in a proper centrifuge and force out those extraneous substances that contaminate its cross-cultural purity.*

I must reiterate that this problem of reification is not merely the problem of the definition of marriage; it is not merely the problem of Gough and Leach. It is inherent in the entire *modus operandi* of the cross-cultural approach in theoretical social anthropology. It is inherent in the controversy over the existence or non-existence of clans, or whether they are clans or lineages, or whether patrilineal clans should be thus called or should be called sibs. It is inherent in the argument over the state and the distinction between acephalous and political societies. It is inherent in the discussions of the difference between magic and religion. One could go on and on.

Statistical Comparisons

Now if we meet such difficulties when we examine in detail specific institutions in a particular setting, it follows that the same problem inheres in every effort to "statisticize" comparisons, and is made worse thereby. Indeed, the only possible way of handling a mass of data statistically in which a comparison of in-

---

* Lévi-Strauss fully appreciates this point, as when he writes "totemism is an artificial unity, existing solely in the mind of the anthropologist, to which nothing specifically corresponds in reality" (1962:10).

stitutions is drawn is to disregard the problem in that form. This was made explicit by David F. Aberle in his analysis of the ecological relationships in matrilineal societies, when he wrote:

Although there were obvious errors in the classification of various cultures [in Murdock's *World Ethnographic Sample*], it was decided not to recode any item of Murdock's tables. If I were to correct only cases which I knew to be in error and were to fail to recheck the remainder, an element of distortion would be introduced into the data. . . . Finally, it was decided not to add new items to the variables coded by Murdock, even if they were important to the investigation, but rather to use certain rough guides to approximate what was needed . . ." (Aberle 1961:671)

Most of the discussion of the validity of statistical comparison has been directed to the nature of the social entity which serves as a unit for statistical analysis, the selection of proper random samples when so few social systems are adequately dealt with, and the attendant problem of cultural "contamination" through diffusion or common cultural history. But these problems are not created by the nature of the data, they derive from problems of method and the need to work statistically. That is, they are only procedural problems, not theoretical or substantive ones. From our viewpoint, the important problem that inheres in the statistical handling of cross-cultural data rests upon the fact that such handling requires the equation of similarly defined institutions from different cultures, where the reality of these equations remains much in doubt; namely, it is the same problem that inheres in all cross-cultural analyses of social institutions: the comparison of incomparables. Indeed, the statistical treatment complicates this problem by the very need for short categorization of complex phenomena into a delimited set of units.

Now Aberle manages to tease out significant correlations between descent, economy, and political units which are interesting, useful, and in general supportive of certain basic ecological assumptions despite the fact that he cannot correct the manifest errors in his data. (His success very probably relates to the fact that he is a sensitive observer better versed in the intricacies of social organization and the character of culture than in the intricacies and character of mathematical manipulations.) It is worth while to let him speak of certain inherent problems in the analysis he undertook. Regarding one of his major variables he writes:

Matriliny consists simply in assigning individuals to kinship categories by reference to descent traced through females. Such categories may be dispersed or localized, organized or unorganized. There may be a dispersed unorganized category, such as a clan, and a localized, organized one, such as a lineage or sub-clan, in the same system. The primary function of the category may be the extension of hospitality and protection, the inheritance of property, mutual defense, redistribution of goods, or authoritative regulation. Or all of these functions may be so important that no one of them can be called primary. When we ask under what conditions matriliny is found, we seem to be attempting to account simultaneously for the conditions which create and those which perpetuate a wide variety of types of units lumped together solely by the pattern of descent reckoning (Aberle 1961:656-657).

A second variable, economic type, which is defined in Murdock's *World Ethnographic Sample* with enough secondary variables to render "the number of combinations enormous," cannot be made to fit any commonsense pattern of economic types, while efforts to use political integration as a variable result in an unbelievable hodgepodge of categories. To some extent these last two points are more critical of Murdock's sampling and coding procedures than they are of the natural bases for classifying the phenomena; nevertheless we know that Murdock is neither naïve nor slipshod, and must therefore assume that the situation reflects a certain recalcitrance of the classification of institutions to fit into meaningful and unified types.

It is surprising that the results of statistical treatment have been as successful as they have, and this fact suggests that the Malinowskian dictum, that each culture must be understood in its own terms, is itself suspect. However, there is another way to read the partial success of statistical investigations of social institutions; namely, that certain social needs repeatedly call forth similar social institutions, that correlations between institutional forms can be found because, broadly speaking, they are the "natural" or "preferred" means by which certain necessary social tasks may best be performed in given circumstances. Or, rather, that the social solutions to functional problems are sufficiently convergent to enable us, the ethnographers, to label them with terms borrowed from other cultures without doing such violence to the actual circumstances as to render invalid the gross analyses we undertake.

Let me conclude this discussion by making it clear what I do and do not mean to imply. First, it should be clear from context that I do not deplore the continued use of functional analysis or statistical treatment of the available data. The former is necessary to the discovery of the depths of human involvement in cultural and social behavior; there is a good deal of the natural history of man that still needs exploration, and therefore the natural history phase of our discipline should not be brought to a premature close. The statistical treatment of social correlates cannot be abandoned, for they are necessary to the demonstration that certain institutional solutions are regularly found to meet the recurrent problems that a society must face under given ecological circumstances.

But neither of these enterprises—functional analysis or statistical treatment—in their existing forms will solve the problems that should be central to the anthropological discipline. They will not solve them because the one is limited in its capacity for extrapolation while the other engages in the falsification of reality. This falsification is obscured by terminological disputes and taxonomic niceties. What is consistent from culture to culture is not the institution; what is consistent are the social problems. What is recurrent from society to society is solutions to these problems.

III

THE CONTEXT
OF SOCIAL SYSTEMS

As we have seen, structural analyses are not amendable to extrapolation whereas comparative analyses are engaged in the false enterprise of comparing incomparables, since institutions are defined on a shifting base of diverse cultures. Comparative functionalism does not commit the former error because it starts with a comparative approach; it does not commit the latter because it does not derive the units of comparison from the cultures themselves.

Where then do we derive the functions which we intend to compare? They must be derived from a model of human behavior; that is, they stem from theory. We cannot, of course, offer a full-fledged model in all its refinements at the outset, but must develop it by constant correction against empirical analyses. Similarly, we do not start with a list of functions drawn up, as I have tried to do (with indifferent results) on a very broad scale (Gold-schmidt, 1959), and which was more elaborately done (but still inadequately) by Aberle *et al.* (1950). Indeed, what will be presented here is not a model in the true sense, but rather a schema for a model, a general plan or program within which the detailed model—or sectors of such a model—can be constructed. I shall, however, refer to it as a model.

The model of society is itself concerned with *social functions;* that is, the actions requisite or desirable for self-maintenance of the social system. These functions will be performed by "institutions," or patterned modes of interaction among the personnel of a society for fulfilling these functions. However, the model must operate within a field, and this field is constituted of three basic parts: (1) the *psychobiological character of man,* (2) the *ecosystem,* and (3) the *temporal dimension.* The first of these has a constant character (so far as we now know); the second has two dimensions of variation, and the third is multivariant.

In this chapter I will develop these contextual aspects of social action; in the next chapter some of the aspects of the organization of social systems.

The Psychobiological Character of Man

As sociologists, we are concerned with the character of society. But we cannot create a model of society without consideration of the nature of the elements out of which it is made, and certainly one of these elements is mankind itself. We have only two choices: either we ignore this problem and insert unrecognized attitudes and attributes into our system by our choice of words and syntax, or we face the issue explicitly and set forth what these elements are —or may be—in our theoretical formulation. Having thus stated the matter, it is self-evident that there really is no choice.

First, we must explore a false problem in sociology: the fear of reductionism. The recognition of the animal aspects of man, or assumptions about man's nature or about human tendencies, do not constitute a reduction of sociological phenomena to the biological level; they do not suggest that social facts are merely the projection onto the community level of psychobiological facts. As sociologists, we are concerned with the differences among patterns of behavior in different populations; psychobiological facts cannot explain these differences because they are themselves constant, not diverse. Yet they are part of the reality within the terms of which social interaction takes place. Nobody denies that biological attributes set a basis for human life; nobody would expect world ethnography to have the same shape if man did not have to eat, if he could reproduce parthenogenetically, if he had no capacity for human speech, if he were not a tool-using creature with requisite hands and eyes, if he were born with full capacity for self-maintenance. The question is not *whether* we recognize the character of man-as-animal underlying the character of social action; it is, rather, *what* attributes must be recognized. Boas appreciated this problem, though in accordance with attitudes then current, when he wrote: "It is . . . one of the fundamental aims of scientific anthropology to learn which traits of behavior, if any, are organically determined and are, therefore, the common property of mankind, and which are due to the culture in which we live" (Boas 1962:206).

This recognition of psychological attributes, it can easily be shown, is regularly found in social anthropological thought. If we say, with Kluckhohn (1944), that magical practices increase where opportunities for overt conflict are suppressed, we are assuming that there is a more or less constant quantum of hostility latent in a population; and futhermore that hostility will find an outlet or make one. If we say that an institution serves the function of reducing in-group conflict, or that a ceremony reinforces identity, we are assuming that human beings have both a tendency toward conflict and a need for symbolic representation of their ego-involvements. We either say this or we are saying that society is somehow making these requirements which it then proceeds to solve—a thesis which reduces functionalism to a meaningless tautology. Yet I do not believe

35

that one can follow the logic of any structural analysis without finding these hidden assumptions, whether they are in the scholar's awareness (as with Kluck-hohn) or not.*

Thus we are making explicit what is usually implicit, but not reducing our explanations to the level of psychobiology, any more than a physiologist who recognizes the problems inherent in the oxidation process is reducing physiology to chemistry. The structure of blood and lungs in an animal cannot be explained by chemistry, but still it cannot be explained without full recognition of the oxidation-reduction process.†

* This was written before I had discovered Anthony F. C. Wallace's neat and economic demonstration, using Radcliffe-Brown as a model, that there is "a certain implicitly psychological viewpoint which even the most unpsychological professors of anthropology have, willy nilly, always maintained" (Wallace 1962:3). It is implicit as well in Lévi-Strauss' treatment with respect to affective behavior, particularly when he discussed Durkheim's reduction of Totemism to "instinctive tendency." But of course similar reductions to biological assumptions—albeit more sophisticated—are resorted to by Lévi-Strauss himself, when he refers to the laws of language "and even the laws of thought" (Lévi-Strauss 1962:70–71, 91).

† The usual falsification of this problem is nowhere better expressed than in an article just come to hand (Kaplan 1965) as this essay goes to press. To Kaplan, reductionism is the total explanation of one level of phenomena by the systematics of an underlying level (e.g., thermodynamics by mechanics; culture by psychology). Since, as he rightly asserts, this cannot be done for an-

Now any involvement with man's nature places us, if we are not careful, directly into the classical dispute between nature and nurture, between biology and culture. But these are false distinctions—even on the lower levels of behavior than that represented by man. For the essence not only of human behavior but of all life is that it is contextual: the manifest character of life substance depends upon the unfolding of an inner capacity in the context of an environmental setting. This is true of such things in life as the expression of genetic structures, of the formation of organs in the embryo, or of the "courting" behavior of birds. Hold constant the genetics and change the context and the result may very well be different

---

thropology, he then argues that this means we can disregard entirely the characteristics of the human animal in our scientific explanations of culture. But surely this is a *non sequitur*, and a fallacy that prevents us from examining the assumptions about psychology that we are making.

On the other hand, the following statement makes clear that there can be a proper rapprochement between anthropology and psychology, and indeed is itself almost the suggestion of an approach of the kind set forth here: "It may be that a single conceptual model, based not upon summary reductionism but upon gradual coalescence, may be created which is usable both for that portion of psychology that deals with the individual interacting with his fellows and with that part of anthropology which deals with the approximations of individuals to cultural forms and with the growth and change of cultures insofar as these arise from individual variation" (Kroeber and Kluckhohn 1963:373-374).

(Baerends, 1958). If ever an Einsteinian formula for behavior is developed, it will be an equation that expresses this relationship between the inner unfolding that we generally think of as genetic, and the external situation which we generally think of as environment, nurture, or (for man) culture. For nothing happens—biologically or socially—without context, while context is nothing without events. Those who study social life should take solace in the recognition of this underlying phenomenon of biological behavior, for thus we are freed of a false problem.

Nor need we be troubled with the distinction between absolutes and mere tendencies, though perhaps this point should be given a moment's thought. For many, if not all, of the postulated characteristics, it will suffice if there is a tendency toward; if there is a significant element of the population that has such a tendency rather than all people at all times. The economist will tell you that the price of oranges is based upon supply and demand, but he does not have to assume that all people like oranges and that everybody is prepared to pay the going price—merely that enough people want oranges sufficiently so that they will forego alternative satisfaction at a given level in order to obtain them. Similarly, Kluckhohn does not have to assume that all people are hostile, but only that there are enough who are sufficiently hostile to create a problem which (under the circumstances) can be resolved only by the indirect outlet of magic.

Though as anthropologists we must make explicit assumptions about the psychobiological aspects of man, we face the problem that these themselves are subject to disagreement among those scholars who are more directly involved with psychology. Though anthropologists cannot claim the expertise to adjudicate among the schools of psychological thought, the fact remains that the ultimate viability of psychological theories relevant to man depends upon their adequately comprehending the diverse forms of human behavior as these are manifested under natural conditions—i.e., the ethnographic facts. As anthropologists, what we must inevitably do—and what we have either implicitly or explicitly been doing—is to shop around among those psychological theories and frames of reference which we believe are necessary in order to make coherent sense out of the events observed in the field. While at first blush this may seem both difficult and inappropriate, it is in fact neither. It is not so difficult because at the macrolevel of psychological understanding and in the limited areas relevant to sociological investigation, the differences in theoretical outlook are not so great as one might assume. It is not inappropriate because the use of models—of hypothetical systems—rests on the basic notion that all elements of the model are tentative. Anthropology serves, thus, as a test of psychological theory in those areas where the latter concerns itself with social behavior.

As the comparative functional approach demands that the psychological assumptions be brought into the open, it is necessary to set forth what I think are the indispensible elements of the system. In this I will not only keep my considerations on a general level—in my later exemplification I will suggest some more specific items—but will keep them at a minimum. For, it seems to me, the anthropologist should go no further into psychological theory than is absolutely demanded for the purposes of his sociological analyses. We need not delay over the self-evident factor of animal needs: food, sexual outlet, infantile dependence, creature comforts. To those elements which man shares with related mammals, we need only add that man differs in his continuous sexual readiness, as distinct from animal responses to the estrous cycle, and the greatly extended period of infantile dependence; but these, too, have been adequately comprehended in the literature. Similarly, we need not pause long over man's peculiar manipulative skill, the hand-eye coordination which makes tool-using possible, which gives man his evolutionary advantage, and renders worth while (in a purely survival sense) the whole business of culture. We might suggest, however, that this may place a higher premium on individual skillfulness (both physical and mental) than is likely to be the case for other forms of life.

The first characteristic of mankind that must be specified is the requirement of humans for human interaction. I have elsewhere termed this "the need for positive affect" (Goldschmidt 1959:26 ff.). Whether this is terminologically satisfactory I leave for others to say, but I am convinced that there is an aspect of man in the interactional area which is universal—a part of the inner drive toward associations—and which is necessary for the very establishment of culture and the maintenance of society. Harlow's experiments with rhesus monkeys suggest that it is not limited to man, and there is no reason why we should assume that it is; though its manifestations seem different in degree, if not in kind, from those interactional demands that make for herds and flocks among nonprimate vertebrates. In a cultured animal, so much more is dependent upon it; in a symbolizing animal, so much more is incorporated in it. It seems inevitable that we shall find in this affect hunger at least some of the motivation for the learning that is essential to culture, and the tie of the individual to community life upon which human survival so firmly depends.

This is, of course, quintessentially an interactional need; it depends upon environment and response. Society is built on it, for in it lies the centripetal force that binds persons together. Developmentally, in each individual it must necessarily have its first expression in the domestic ménage, in the mother-child relationship and the extension of interpersonal interaction to ever wider circles of kindred and community. Whether this extension of interaction follows patterns laid down by Erikson (1963: chaps. 2 and 7) is beyond my competence to determine; the very least that can be said of his presentation is that it offers us a basis for examining cross-culturally the relation between the inborn tendencies and their social expression.*

Human interaction is thus seen as being, at one and the same time, a need of man and a requisite for society; it has therefore a particular and crucial involvement in the very relation between the individual (and hence psychology) and the community (and hence sociology). As I see it, the individual is primarily motivated toward his own physical self-perpetuation and his symbolic self-aggrandizement, yet both of these can be achieved only through deep dependence and involvement with others. There thus is inherent in every man-in-society an essential dualism, which is a *leitmotif* in many cultures and most philosophies. This dualism lies at the very roots of human action, and places in all men, in all cultures, an internal conflict that is perduring and inescapable.†

The second major characteristic is truly and un-

---

* Erikson has recently endeavored to extend his concept of developmental stages into the sociological sphere by showing their several contributions to ritualized behavior. This is found in a provocative essay which demonstrates the kind of rapprochement that must take place between psychological and sociological theory (Erikson 1965).

† "Human culture is established through a series of renunciations. The sacrifice of self is the beginning of personality" (Rieff 1959, as quoted by Caudill 1962).

questionably unique in man: his capacity for symbol-ization. While any evolutionary hypothesis about man's origins would lead us to expect some kind of antecedent in other forms of life, it is quite clear that man's capacity in this direction is of an entirely new order. We take this to be the essential human mental endowment which makes language possible (and which is therefore necessary to true culture) but our concern here goes beyond the facts of language. For unfortunately man's use of symbols does not limit itself to the business of verbal communication; symbols pervade every aspect of his life activities. In fact it is better to say that man lives his life in a symbolic universe, for all reality is mediated in the form of symbols; the symbol serves as the measure of goals for self-aggrandizement and the standard by which personal needs are fulfilled. The dominance of the cerebrum in the human brain over the "gut satisfactions" of the hind brain has its counterpart in the dominance of the symbol system in human society over creature comforts and physical satisfactions.

There is another aspect of man's mental endowment that is closely associated with his symbolizing character; namely, his tendency to taxonomize.* Language, by its very nature, requires that speakers treat *categories* of phenomena, that they recognize tree-

* "The use of taxonomic systems is not confined to librarians and biologists; it is a fundamental principle of human thinking" (Frake 1962:81).

ness and distinguish it from bush-ness, that they recognize adult-ness and distinguish it from child-ness, that they render the infinite variety of human experiences into a finite series of categories, treated as units. The linguists long ago showed us that different languages taxonomize the world differently, which is only to substantiate that there is an arbitrariness to any taxonomic system. But this tendency to create classes of objects is itself a quality of mind which has particular sociological significance—as we know from kinship studies.

In this discussion of man's symbolizing tendency we should take special note of the fact that the self also becomes a symbolic object, that the individual in a symbolic world is himself a symbol. This is the key to the fact that human motivation cannot be understood satisfactorily in terms of the gratification of animal needs, but only in terms of the symbolic reference in which these motivations are operative. That the individual is himself a symbol is also relevant to a universal distinction in human societies between *me* and *thee*, and the extension of this distinction to *mine* and *thine*. Above all, it is this ambiance of cultural symbolization in human communities that prevents ethnology from being merely a branch of ethology.

A third element that should be introduced is the fact of human differentiation. Individuals have different capacities to perform the different tasks which they face in self-maintenance, and this reality must be appreciated and must also enter into any calculations of a social system, for the social system must take account of this natural diversity. Let me be clear what I don't mean by this, lest it be misunderstood. I don't mean that one ethnic group is genetically intellectually better than or different from another, but that in any ethnic group there will be a range of capacities, and this becomes a social fact in its own right. I also don't mean that some people are naturally "better" than others, but only that some will be stronger, some will be fleeter, some will be calmer, some will be better able to withstand pain. These traits will not, of course, necessarily run together. One of the unfortunate aspects of our thinking on this subject has been the lumping together of a variety of undefined traits in such a general measure as "I.Q."

We must accept the fact that there are differences between the sexes, a fact of life that anthropologists have tended to overlook in their false equalitarianism. I do not mean, again, to differentiate on a value-laden basis, but to recognize differentiation as such. Anthropological quibbles to the contrary, there is a considerable degree of uniformity in the division of labor between the sexes, a degree of uniformity that cannot be shunted off as historic accident. Only rarely, if ever, are there exceptions to the following: men do the hunting of game, the caring for herds, engage in military activity, and are in control of political life; it is men who exchange for women, not women for men; women care for the children, maintain the domestic ménage, do the cooking of staple foods. The correlations are so high that it behooves us to examine the exceptions, rather than to disregard the generalizations, as we have been wont to do. It is unfortunate that the affirmation of these differences is unnecessarily involved with our own value judgments, for it tends to obscure the important fact for social life. Whether these reflect differences in the quality of intellect (as was once generally believed), in patterns of hormonal balance, or in the necessitous division of cultural labor as a complement to the division of biological labor that marks the sexes, the *fact* of difference is itself significant. We cannot understand the character of social systems without adequately taking into account the cultural response to sexual differentiation.

Human behavior is learned behavior to an entirely different degree than is true of other animals, so that the learning processes must be appreciated; especially an understanding of reward and punishment in learning, the importance of reinforcement and the like. But what is especially to be recognized is that man's learning involves the symbolic world in which he lives, that rewards and punishments, reinforcement and extinction, all relate to the world as mediated in the existing symbol system of his community and, except perhaps for small infants, never are simply operative on the gut level of behavioral needs.

Having said this, however, it is also necessary to make quite clear that the symbol systems, the symbolic values and culturally established goals, are not entirely detached from man's biological requirements. When one examines the diverse prestige symbols in diverse human communities, he is first impressed with their variety and apparent arbitrariness. When, however, one examines them more closely in context, he finds that they generally relate either directly or indirectly (and often symbolically as well) to the satisfaction derived from sex, food, and freedom from pressures of work (Goldschmidt 1953).

It seems worth while here to remind ourselves that man is not the only social animal. We know something now—all too little, to be sure—of the sociology of other species which regularly operate in close communities. Ethologists' observations suggest that there are inter-individual stimuli that evoke regularized behavioral responses among species studied—a psychobiological phenomenon which may well be considered the basis for human institutional behavior.

We see evidence of dominance–submission patterns and we know that, in varying degrees, the constituent members are able to communicate with one another. At the same time, there is a vast difference between these systems and those of even the most primitive

47

THE CONTEXT OF SOCIAL SYSTEMS

human social system known to ethnology. This means that the social phenomena we observe in man cannot be related simply to the fact of social existence; they must relate to the character of man as well. We do not impute hostility-reduction institutions to beehives or symbolization ceremonies to cattle herds. Animal aggregates, even those biologically very close to man, exist without these institutional devices against which we project our functional theses, though they do have simpler "institutions," such as pecking orders.* Inasmuch as other social animals live in aggregates without social institutions, human institutions cannot be understood merely as a response to the fact that our species lives in aggregates. Rather, social institutions must be seen as mechanisms which enable the active collaboration of personnel, in both the material and symbolic contexts in which man lives.

It may be necessary to reiterate here the point, now firmly established in anthropology, that nothing that is biological in man is ever *merely* biological. All creature characteristics that enter into human action are involved in man's symbolic system; i.e., in cultural interpretation. It is hard to think of any single physi-

---

* There is a tendency for ethologists to use terms like "ritual" for descriptions of certain forms of interactional behavior among the lower animals; we must not let this confuse us into assuming that there are symbolic meanings to such actions.

cal activity—heartbeat, respiration rate, eye-blinking, salivation, coughing, dreaming, adrenalin secretion— which remains uninfluenced by the cultural and social system within which the person is operating. But to point out the cultural involvement is not to deny the biological reality (or the biological function) of the physiological element. It is, rather, to reaffirm that everything available to man's consciousness may, and probably always does, get into his symbol system.

In sum, we urge the discontinuation of the nature versus nurture, innate versus learned controversy, and the adoption of a recognition that there are characteristic human urges and potentialities that are channelized through the cultural process and that can be expressed only in the context of a culturally defined institutional system. This means that we must test cross-culturally for such postulated urges and potentials to examine whether they are universal or sporadic, whether they may be completely suppressed or merely submerged, under what circumstances they may be handled in particular ways and what the consequences for social life are when they are handled in such ways. Exemplifications of this approach will be given in the next chapter.

Ecosystem

As I stated earlier, each society operates as a system in the context of other systems, and we turn now to the environmental circumstances in which society operates, and which is here called the ecosystem. This environmental context impinges upon man because it offers the opportunities which man can exploit for the satisfaction of his needs, and the circumstances he must cope with in order to sustain himself.

It is necessary to distinguish two aspects of the ecosystem: (1) the physical environment of climate, topography, soils, flora, and fauna that make up the landscape in which the society operates, and (2) the surrounding social systems of other human communities which impinge upon the society, either because of its geographical propinquity or its social interrelationships.

There is not much that needs to be said about the physical environment, for its importance has generally been recognized, but a few points deserve reiteration. First, environment offers up those material things out of which people can build their lives; it creates problems against which people must build defenses, or toward which action has to be directed. Second, it is the essential characteristic of the cultural mode of life that man can alter this environment in terms of needs; he shapes the stone, he warms himself by the fire, he builds a shelter against sun or wind, he trades for goods not locally available, and so on. Yet man's alteration of this environment is limited; it is an external system with which his ingenuity as engineer and sociologist must cope. Third, the environment does not always mean the same thing; its potentialities differ in relation to human knowledge of how to exploit the advantages or cope with the difficulties. From the sociological point of view it is important to appreciate first that this environment differs in terms of the accumulated knowledge of the people who constitute the society, and second, that its exploitation is carried on through social institutions which therefore must inevitably relate in some degree to this external system.

Even more important as a factor in any social system is the social environment in which it operates. This can vary from being completely absent, as in the case of Arctic Eskimo society (whose members were not aware of any other humans on earth when they were first encountered by Europeans) to societies heavily dominated by the surrounding social environment. Indeed, the recognition of this factor makes it possible for us to study social systems which are themselves parts of larger social systems, it being of the greatest importance to appreciate the dynamic relationship between the system under study and its social environment.

This factor, once mentioned, is so self-evidently important that it is a wonder that so little recognition has been taken of it in sociological investigation. In truth, except for a few isolated communities, such as those of the Eskimo, it is a factor of first importance in all societies. Perhaps the most dramatic importance under primitive circumstances is the potentiality of hostile relationships. The influence of warfare on cultural development in historic societies is generally appreciated by the historians; it is equally a factor in primitive circumstances.* This is not merely a matter of architecture and armament; it is also a matter of institutional arrangements for protection or exploitation.† The existence of weak neighbors is influential on the institutions of those societies that are powerful

---

* A classic example of this problem is found in the monograph by Frank Secoy on Plains Indian history (Secoy 1953), and developed by S. C. Oliver in his more recent study, "Ecology and Cultural Continuity as Contributing Factors in the Social Organization of the Plains Indian" (Oliver 1961). E. V. Winans (1965) has also shown how Hehe life patterns were influenced by the changing character of their tribal neighbors. Sahlins (1961) makes the same general point—though on more doubtful evidence—in his comparison between Nuer and Tiv segmentary systems.

† Even so perceptive a student of society as Aberle appears not to appreciate the vital importance of this aspect of social life as an influence on the structuring of society. In a later chapter I will show that the Nayar pattern of interpersonal relationships makes sense only in terms of the military function of the Nayar castes. A similar situation was found among the matrifocal Cossacks of pre-nineteenth-century Russia (Tolstoy, 1949). But in his comparative essay, Aberle (1961) takes no cognizance of the environment of neighboring societies, and when he calls for more ecologic considerations in Murdock's *World Ethnographic Sample*, he makes no mention of this aspect of ecology (Aberle 1961:724–725).

and exploitative, just as much and as surely as the powerful neighbors influence the institutions of those who try only to protect themselves. But warfare (though probably the most important) is not the only aspect of the social environment institutions must cope with or societies find advantageous. There is, for example, the opportunity for trade, for enrichment of the total potential of each environment through mutual exchange of goods. There is also the borrowing of knowledge, the recognition of alternative life modes, the problem of protecting one's own identity against others, and many other effects upon a society that may result from the fact that it is in an environment constituted of other social systems.

The Temporal Dimension

Man lives in a time continuum; that is, present behavior is made up out of past experience and is projected into the future. It is impossible to understand any social system without taking this "cultural heritage"—as it is generally called—into account. Thus, we must appreciate the dimension of time and the fact of cultural continuity as an element of the field within which each society operates: Every social system has a past and is directed to the future. Out of its past it derives the knowledge and patterns of behavior that we call culture, and its actions are designed to project the system into the future, to make for continuity. As anthropologists we take this for granted, and often make this the major orientation of our work. As sociologists, however, we concern ourselves with the ongoing events at a moment of time, so that we have stopped the action to see internal relationships. Nevertheless, these internal relationships cannot be comprehended without an appreciation of this temporal dimension, though for our purposes we are leaving it outside our central considerations and treating it as a "field" within which the social system must operate. As sociologists, we are interested primarily in the patterns of human interaction; but as these relate on the one hand to man's needs and capacities, and on the other to the environmental potential, we must give some attention to the techniques—the instruments, experience, and knowledge—which the society has for the exploitation of this environment. For it matters a great deal to the potential forms that institutions may take—the advantages and disadvantages of alternate possibilities—if we know whether the culture knows only hunting game and gathering wild products, or if the people are able to dig irrigation ditches and have electric-powered pumps. That is to say, the exploitative technology is an element in man's relation to his dual environment, and must enter into any consideration of the institutional instrumentalities by which man wrests his livelihood from the environment. For technical knowledge is not—or has not been until recent years—freely available to all peoples on the globe. It has grown by gradual accretions of information from simple beginnings, and various peoples for a variety of reasons have had a greater or a lesser amount of this knowledge in their cultural heritage. This is not the place to expand on this evolutionary aspect of human knowledge; all that must be asserted at the moment is that the level of such knowledge is an element in the structural situation of each society, for it is through this knowledge that it exploits its environmental potential.

The cultural past has similar implications for the institutional machinery of a society. No peoples create institutions *de novo;* all build their structures out of materials existing in their cultural heritage. They may dampen down one element and elevate another; they may shift functions of existing institutions as needs arise, but they do not, and they cannot, disregard their past. If this is true for modern social engineering, we may well assume it is true for the less self-conscious sociologizing of primitive peoples.

At this juncture we have not as yet got to our model of society, but have established only the context in which all societies must operate: the "field" in the Lewinian sense. This field has three elements: (1) the biologically established character of the human animal, (2) the physical and social environment within which every society operates, and (3) the temporal dimension through which it acquires the paraphernalia of its existence (its culture) and through which it projects its continuity into the future (its evolutionary thrust).

IV

SCHEMA FOR
A MODEL OF SOCIETY

The cultural mode of life presents difficulties to the human animal that do not seem to beset less intellectual creatures; nevertheless, from a purely survival point of view it has a twofold advantage: (1) it enables man to develop and pass on complex forms of behavior involving tools and weapons with which he feeds and protects himself, and (2) it enables man to collaborate for mutual assistance and protection in large organized entities. It is the manner in which he does the latter that is the particular subject of the social anthropologist's attention, and which will be examined in some detail in this chapter. It is the evolutionary role of this human characteristic that enables us to call elements of social organization "instrumentalities." This instrumental role leads to the notion of functional requisite and to the recognition that some solutions to the problems created by the very existence of social life may be more satisfactory than others.

In this chapter, therefore, it is my task to indicate the manner in which social functions are to be seen. It is not my intent to conjure up some list of functional requisites, a task which I have already specifically eschewed, but rather to examine the character of society in such a way as to suggest the kinds of functional elements which should be sought and the manner of seeking them.

Broadly speaking, we can recognize two general classes of functions:

(1) The first class of functions are those relating directly to human needs: obtaining food, providing shelter, procreating and the nurture of the dependent infants, protection against external threats, and the transmission of requisite knowledge. Essentially these are the animalistic requirements of man (as transformed by cultural definition), and must be performed by any living creature with similar physical characteristics, but in human communities some or all of them are regularly performed by supra-familial groups.

(2) But as man performs these functions in collaboration, he also has a second set of functional requisites; namely, the provision of the institutional machinery to maintain the social system as a system, in order to prevent the society from being rent by the centrifugal tendencies of individual self-interest. That is, the society must institutionalize behavior,

form collaborative groups and maintain their internal harmony, and harness the individual to community action.*

In this context, it is useful to think of human society as that system of organization which mediates between the psychobiological drives of the individual on the one hand and the resources out of which life is sustained and protected on the other, utilizing the techniques that the community is heir to. This very important aspect of social organization relates it to the several fields within which, as we have shown, it must operate. At the same time human society must also be seen as the means by which the ego-centered psychobiological needs of the individual are both given satisfaction and held in check, for these ego-oriented needs—whether they be food and protection, sexual gratification, or personal self-satisfaction —can only be attained by man in a social interaction system. This aspect of social organization has been least well attended by anthropologists, though manifestly it is of first importance to the understanding of any social system.†

* Kroeber and Kluckhohn (1963:110) criticize the "functional" definition of culture for its emphasis upon problem-solving or need-fulfilling orientation, "for culture creates problems as well as solving them." The comparative functional approach explicitly recognizes the interaction between need-fulfilling and need-creating aspects of social (i.e., cultural) behavior.

† Gluckman is perhaps the outstanding spokesman for the recognition of conflict in society. His stance, however,

The fundamental quality of human behavior as distinct from that in nonhuman societies is that action is not random, it does not consist of individuals eating or couples mating or aggregates hunting, but that these things are done according to regularized patterns which are provided by the social environment and adhered to more or less faithfully by all normal members of the community.* It is necessary for social

---

is far removed from the position expressed here, inasmuch as he sees the social expression of conflict as being created by society, by custom; not inherent in social relations *per se.* Thus he writes: "a community is always elaborately divided and cross-divided by customary allegiance; and the elaboration is aggravated by what is most specifically a production of man in society: his religion and ritual" (1959:1). And, again, "Custom similarly accentuates the difference between parent and child" (1959:54–55). Because Gluckman sees conflict as created by custom, not inherent in the quintessential human relationship, he cannot understand his own conflict with Monica Wilson over whether certain ritual acts are rebellious or confessional. This he makes clear in his concluding remarks on their dispute: "In short, I hope I have now made clear that I was not dealing with psychical conflict, but with social conflict: conflict arising from discrepancy and conflict of laws, conflict of interests and social processes, conflict of state unity and territorial dispersion, etc. This is why I did not use the term Oedipus complex" (1959:27).

* It is of course true that in animal communities the immediate intent of the animals is communicated to their fellows by more or less standardized signals for such purposes as the maintenance of boundaries or of peace, the

interaction to be formalized so that in any normal situation a person will be able to anticipate the acts of others. A simple example suffices: despite some acrimonious transatlantic discussion, it matters not one whit whether people drive on the right or on the left side of the road, but it is a matter of life and death that one or the other be the regular way of driving. We may say, then, that normal social intercourse of any kind whatsoever must be *institutionalized* and that a society cannot survive, nor its members tolerate, the continued absence of such institutionalization.

The word institution has given students of society difficulty (often expressed by avoidance). I shall use it here only very loosely as a noun, but more precisely as a verb. That is, I will as a matter of convenience speak of institutions of marriage, family, government, and the like, without trying to specify the metes and bounds of such entities, for they are not discrete, bounded items.* But as a verb, institutionali-

---

establishment of dominance, mutual collaboration, and the like. It is perhaps specifically the construction by humans of symbolic meaning to these acts which has enabled them to endure and which gives them the dimension of institutionalization. It is precisely when these meanings break down in social patterns that we evoke the figure of speech of animal behavior, as for instance, "the asphalt jungle."

* Indeed, the essence of my argument thus far has been that efforts at a precise use of the concepts of institution have been a hampering influence on comparative studies.

zation refers to the process of organizing acts, attitudes, feelings, and interpersonal relationships into regularized patterns given sanction by the symbol system of the culture. This usage is supported I think, by Radcliffe-Brown who writes: "The established norms of conduct of a particular form of social life it is usual to refer to as *institutions*. An institution is an established norm of conduct recognized as such by a distinguishable social group or class of which therefore it is an institution. The institutions refer to a distinguishable type or class of social relationships and interactions" (Radcliffe-Brown 1952:10).*

There is an element of feedback in any social system which helps us understand the process of institutionalization. In the symbolic world of social behavior, the truth of a proposition is regularly self-validated by the consensus that it is true. This is what Merton (1948) called "the self-fulfilling prophecy," but which I prefer to call the self-validation of cultural assumptions. Thus, the value of money depends not only upon the consensus that the money has value, but upon the regular action in the community that treats it with such a value, so that the grocer's being willing to treat my dollar as having a

---

However, a loose nominal use remains, indispensable for discourse.

* Though he provides a nominal definition, the essence of that definition lies in process.

dollar's worth in terms of his commodities makes it sensible for me to accept that dollar for an appropriate quantum of my time at work. How such systems come into being is itself a vexatious problem, which we cannot treat in the present context, but we do see such symbols being destroyed from time to time. For these symbolic truths are true only when a community acts upon them.* A community may cease to do so because external elements of truth may intrude themselves—as, for example, the doctrine of the divine right of kings or more recently the promulgation of Lamarckian heritability of acquired characteristics as promulgated under Stalinist Russia by Lysenko—or because sentiments shift. The emperor did not, after all, continue to enjoy his invisible cloak.

Now this characteristic of social life is of prime importance, and must be given some attention. It raises philosophical problems of a difficult nature, for no other substance regularly subjected to scientific inquiry is involved with this self-propelled causative

* Certain psychic disorders are characterized by the fact that the individual's system of symbols, however real to himself, is not shared by the community and therefore is "unreal" in the social world. In some states the law, in practice, distinguishes between the leaders of a religious cult and a psychopath by specifying some minimum number of acceptors of his system; i.e., a social definition of his private symbolic world.

force. If we say that a society has values and that these values, whatever they may be, orient the individuals toward a certain kind of behavior, we raise to a level of causation a force which, in itself, is a product of the consensus of the very people who are thus motivated. Thus, social causation has a strange metaphysical property not shared by similar "forces" in nature. However that may be, we cannot fail to recognize the reality of the symbolic world to which the individual is always a creature, and of which he is, in some measure, a creator.

Let us next examine the dimensions of society as an environment, and later turn to the character of society as seen from the standpoint of the individual. It seems useful to distinguish these elements in a social system: (1) groups, (2) patterns of status and role, and (3) values.

The work of society (that is, the first of the two general kinds of functions discussed at the beginning of this chapter) is accomplished largely in the context of groups. It is not quite accurate to say that a society is merely constituted of social groups, for there are also dyadic personal relations, or relations between persons and groups, but it is proper to say (1) that all societies involve a multiplicity of groups, (2) these groups are structured so as to interrelate, and (3) group structures and group interrelationships are essential to the operation of all social systems. (One is tempted to say that groups are to society what the cell is to a life form, but the analogy is incorrect in many particulars, not the least of which is the fact that groups can operate within larger groups, or in a manner cross-cutting to other groups.) Groups may be of any size. They have certain common features:

1) a personnel;
2) a boundary, a distinction between members and nonmembers;
3) an internal structure which (a) defines role relationships among the personnel, and (b) organizes action;
4) a symbolic formulation;
5) a patterned external relationship;
6) a function, in the sense that they meet a felt need for their own personnel, or serve some necessary functions for society as a whole, or both.

Within groups, and within society as a whole, it is necessary to define the positions and actions of individuals in such a way that they themselves have a clear notion of their obligations and rights in any normal situation. Thus a series of statuses is defined which involves patterns of expectation and which any incumbent will normally perform in accordance with his own talents and according to his personal style.

Finally, there are the shared values of the community, the patterns of behavior, the qualities of action, the social positions, and the symbolic representations for such qualities, which are a part of the consensus. These values (or some of them) may be held in common or may express subcultural diversity; they may be explicitly different for different sectors of the community (males versus females, adults versus children, priests versus laymen, and so on) and still be shared in the sense that such behavior is expected of persons, according to their proper roles, by the whole community.

At this point the temporal aspect of social systems needs to be reiterated. The groups, the statuses and roles, the values of any one moment are the product of a heritage that has been transmitted out of the past and modified in the course of events by individual acts and circumstances. It is this continuity from the past that makes possible the continuous existence of a value system to which each individual must subordinate himself even though, in time, he may alter (or reinforce) that value system for others.* The groups into which the individual enters existed before him and continue beyond his incumbency into the future. For it is important that a society not only has a past but also has a future, or the anticipation of a future, which is relevant to the present.

* It is thus that the individual is molded by the reality of an ongoing symbol system which he unwittingly accepts, and which at one point in time is external to him, while at a later point in time he is reinforcing it, and perhaps reinterpreting it, for others.

The implications of a social order cannot be understood unless it is examined from the standpoint of the individual, for, as I have already stated, the social order mediates between the personal needs of the individual and the sources of their fulfillment. That in the process these needs are transformed into desires, that they are redefined in cultural terms, that they sometimes contravene physiological needs, these things do not impair the essential validity of this statement.

We have come too much to think that the infant enters society as a completely plastic entity, a *tabula rasa* onto which the culture imprints his ultimate character. The plasticity of the infant is limited; he has his own inner dynamic, and is a striving, demanding, manipulating, and controlling piece of life, tamed by the community into some modicum of conformity. But he never divests himself of this self-interest; he merely channelizes it into the appropriate behavior (if he is to be at all successful) for his particular time and place. There is inherent in each individual a conflict between himself and his community, a conflict which internalizes itself as a duality, which however much it may be subordinated in the manifest aspects of social life is never entirely resolved. What is more important, from a sociological point of view, is that it is often structured into social action—a point to which I want to return shortly.

Nor, of course, does the individual come into his

society naked of social identifications; rather, he is normally endowed with some memberships, some group identifications, some expectations with respect to status and role which, like the latent images on a film, are developed when the proper age and circumstances arise. Thus some aspects of the personal self of each individual are preordained by the context of his birth, and provide that self with symbolic meanings for him from the outset. Beyond this, there are roles to be played. These he may play well or badly (in terms of his community's evaluation of how they should be played), and he receives rewards and punishments in accordance with how he plays them. These may involve gratification of his physical needs for food, grooming and other comforts, but they also involve (and this in early infancy as well as throughout life) those satisfactions to his ego which assist in the development of a symbolic self, with such positive and negative valences as his behavior-in-context provides.

I want to make clear that I am not here juxtaposing either of two classic oppositions: man versus society or biological versus cultural needs. I am, rather, saying that the individual has both a set of personal biologically derived needs and a set of personal culturally derived needs, and that the two are inextricably intertwined and interrelated; furthermore, that each of them can only be satisfied in the context of community action. The one because that is the way the economic work of the world of man is performed, the other because socially desired needs (directly concerned as they are with the self-image) can be satisfied only by and through a public. The conflict between individual and society, therefore, is not literally a contest of the one against the many but is an internalized conflict between two aspects of the personal life—one centered on the self as an object of direct gratification, the other a recognition that this self can only be gratified through the satisfaction of others. The ego-centered appetites may be libidinal or hedonistic, but they may equally be for status, approval, power, or control. Nor is social approval inherently antagonistic to libidinal satisfaction, as our Protestant-oriented culture tends to think. The two may be in substantial harmony, as in expressions of *machismo* in Mexico or the qualities of "negritude" in West Africa.

Every society provides markers by which the individual can rate his symbolic self; that is, with culturally defined values (and their symbolic representation). The values may be individual- or group-oriented; they may be ascriptional or achieved; they may be consistent or mutually contradictory, continuous and self-reinforcing, or discontinuous and anxiety provoking. It is in their terms, however, that the individual is forced to act if he is to gratify that

69

symbolic self which, one may say, he moves through life and into the future, in accordance with the established rules of his community.

While the individual must pick his way through the thicket of cultural expectations, personal gratifications, and physical satisfactions, the view from the other side is different. For the society, the task vis-à-vis the individual is to provide him with a satisfactory self-image, while, at the same time, preventing his personal impulses from disrupting the integrity of the community and the needs of the group, against which they stand as a threat. The culture must, so to speak, institutionalize the internal disharmony that inheres in each individual. It is a delicate, if not entirely impossible, task and I am not so surprised at its recurrent failures as at its apparent frequent success, or—to avoid an all-or-none phrasing of the issue—at the frequency with which a viable balance is maintained.

If, as I believe, this internalized conflict is inherent in the social situation, if it is a built-in feature of man-in-society, then it follows that the task of every society is to provide the institutional means of handling (and I don't mean of resolving) this conflict. That there are many roads to the achievement is a basic truth learned from ethnography. But two aspects must be recognized: (1) that adequate achievement of this end varies in terms of the circumstances in which the society operates, so that a successful solution in one instance is a poor one in another; and (2) that societies do not handle the problem with equal degrees of satisfaction for the personnel involved, or for the purposes of self-maintenance of the society itself.

Let us consider the first problem briefly. We might exemplify the point by reference to the classic comparison between the Pueblo and Northwest Coast Indians, not in terms of the value judgments that Benedict (1934) rendered in *Patterns of Culture*, but with consideration for the demands placed upon individuals in the respective economic system. For surely a people engaged in the dangerous but rewarding business of seafaring that characterizes Kwakiutl life must internalize a high sense of fortitude, a strong independence of action, and a quality of derring-do which are all most inappropriate for the Pueblos, crowded together for protection and forced to save, share, and restrain their impulses if life is to be maintained under the daily drudgery of their arid environment. That the ideological systems are different is clearly a situational demand, and there is no little evidence that failure to restrain impulses among the Hopi and other Pueblos has had deleterious—if not disastrous—results in the past.*

* I am currently engaged in an extensive and detailed analysis of cultural and social adaptation as between hoe-farming and pastoralism in East Africa, and am encouraged from preliminary examination of the data that similar kinds

The second point, that societies handle this problem with differential degrees of success, is less easily demonstrated. I think, however, that we can point up the contrast by examining two cultures operating on roughly the same plane of social advancement—one in which there is a clear institutionalization not only of the demands society makes but of the internalized conflict, and the other where the opposite is the case. First, I shall turn to the Tallensi, using Meyer Fortes' (1959) brief work, *Oedipus and Job in West African Religion*, for it demonstrates the points I wish to make even though Fortes' own major thesis is more clever than it is convincing.

The Tallensi, as all will recall, have a classic patrilineal segmentary lineage system. This means that each individual articulates to the social order through the father and, in a very real sense, the father is therefore the symbolic representation to the individual of the society as a whole—a symbolization clearly expressed in the religious ideology and ritual activity associated with the ancestor cult. Tallensi attitudes toward the father are ambivalent, if not hostile, and this, if Fortes' repeated statements are to be accepted, despite the fact that parental attitudes are essentially warm and friendly.*

of attitudinal and psychological adaptation to such situational demands are to be found.

* Thus Fortes writes: "Now paternal authority, however conscientiously or benevolently exercised, as it usually is

The father is the controlling force in the community; he has absolute authority over his sons; it is in him that the symbolic representations of the restraints of society "naturally" reside. But the society offers a number of institutional devices to contain this conflict, of which the primary ones are the strict avoidance relationship between father and sons,* the demands of the ancestor cult as a continuing projection of this relationship into the future, the externalizing of the symbolic self in terms of a personal shrine which makes demands upon both the son and the father, and the funerary demands which serve (at the very least) to expiate the son's guilt for what we may presume to be a regular wish of death against the controlling and subordinating father. What I believe the Tallensi do is to create an order which is strong in its restraints upon the individual but with the conflict satisfactorily resolved by the individual through its externalization and symbolization. The general internal conflict is not denied, it is not swept under the rug but, rather, is given a high degree of explicitness and then coped with in those terms.

Fortes makes it quite clear that the conflict be-

---

among the Tallensi, inevitably gives rise to expressed hostility and opposition in sons" (1959:27). The point is reiterated, with the same note of surprise, several times.

* "The hostility that this might generate is drained away in the ritual avoidances binding on the eldest son (who represents all his brothers)" (Fortes 1959:31).

tween father and son, which is the central relationship in the whole society, is given explicit philosophic and institutionalized treatment. The ancestor cult, he writes, "is much more than a mnemonic for regulating their social relations. It is the religious counterpart of their social order, hallowing it, investing it with a value that transcends mundane interests and providing for them the categories of thought and belief by means of which they direct and interpret their lives and actions. . . . The ancestor cult is the transposition to the religious plane of the relationships of parents and children; and that is what I mean by describing it as the ritualization of filial piety" (Fortes 1959:29–30). And, finally: "Ultimate responsibility is projected outside the living body politic, not onto neighbors or kinsfolk or natural phenomena, as happens in societies with extensive witchcraft and magical beliefs. . . . What ancestor-worship provides is an institutionalized scheme of beliefs and practices by means of which men can accept some kind of responsibility for what happens to them and yet feel free of blame for failure to control the vicissitudes of life" (Fortes 1959:61).

Now this is not merely the handling of a specific interpersonal relationship; it is that and far more, for the father (as point of articulation and as the central instrument of social reward and punishment, both in the physical and symbolic spheres) is in fact the internalized representation of society and its demands upon the individual Tallensi.

Not every social system makes these matters so clear, nor does every ethnographer have the sensitivity to make the observations. Many societies place greater emphasis upon the uses of brute force, while others, as Fortes suggests, let these emotions be expressed in witchcraft with its potentially disruptive effects. One might be tempted to suggest, in the pattern of the older personality-and-culture tradition, that in the Tallensi case the hostility between father and son was created by the culture in its child-rearing patterns, and that the culture then proceeded to resolve that hostility. But that would be to miss the major point, which is that the demands of society must be focused in some institutionalized relationship; in this instance they are focused on the father-son relationship, and this being the case, they are handled in a manner both acceptable to the individual and functionally efficient for the society. While an older "culture and personality" literature might express surprise at the fact that hostility exists between father and son despite the quality of domestic sentiments, I feel that the Tallensi parent is able to be kind and benevolent precisely because the natural conflict is so satisfactorily institutionalized.

Fortes rightly contrasts the Tallensi with societies riven by witchcraft and sorcery, for it is a reasonable

hypothesis that a prevalence of witches is one response to an institutional system that inadequately
manipulates the internal conflict characterizing man
in society. In this context it is worth while to reexam-
ine Dobuan society (Fortune 1963), since it is the
classic example of a sorcery-ridden community.
There is no need to expand here upon the disorgan-
ized and disoriented character of the social system,
which not only has been presented by Fortune but
was dramatized and publicized by Benedict. It may be
recalled that the society is organized into villages
made up of matrilineages (*susu*) which are matrilineally interrelated, and that marriage is exogamous to
the village but, because of the intense hostility between marital partners and their families, residence
fluctuates regularly between the villages of the husband and wife and, furthermore, the visiting spouse is
kept outside village affairs. Fortune says simply:
"One marries into a village of enemies, witches and
sorcerers . . ." (1963:23). In this society "no con-
ciliatory mechanisms exist" (7), leadership emerges
as a rare happenstance (84), there are no moral
sanctions against adultery, theft, or witchcraft (78),
and "there are no social forms of hostility, only very
real private feelings of the type that cannot be discussed in public" (23). This is a dismal picture of
anarchy, suspicion, and hatred.

Fortune gives us a good deal of information about
the relation between a boy and his father. It is clear

that many institutional devices exist to prevent any close identification between a man and his father, the foremost of which is the hostility felt in the father's village (to which the son has limited access while the father is alive and none whatsoever after the father dies), and the frequency of divorce which apparently breaks all ties. Fortune summarizes this relationship as follows:

[The son] goes every alternate year with his parents to the father's village. There with his mother he is one of Those-resulting-from-Marriage, a stranger, in relation to the Owners, careful never to utter an Owner's personal name. He is a member of the marital grouping as opposed to the *susu* grouping in that village. He has the one advantage that we have seen the marital grouping has over the *susu*—he is a member of the unit that lives in a common house. The marital grouping again goes gardening together—children with their mother and father. In the course of this everyday life in common it normally occurs that a great measure of affection springs up between father and child as well as between mother and child. The affection between mother and child is more stable than that between father and child because divorce is common. In case of divorce the mother-child association continues. The father-child association in such cases is cut short abruptly, for the father avoids his former wife, and since the children remains with her he can only see them infrequently when they are detached from their mother and come to visit him. If he acquires stepchildren by a new marriage he does not care for them sentimentally as if they were his own, if they are at all grown and independent. Nevertheless, in many cases a father remains with his wife and children until some, at least, of his children have won affection from him. There are many things that he cannot provide for his children. His village land, his personal name, his skull, his status, his village palms, and fruit trees he cannot by any possibility alienate from his sister's child in favour of his own child. In all these things his child is Boundary Man in reality as well as in name (1963:14–15).

In a matrilineal society, of course, it is the mother's brother with whom the child is expected to identify and from whom he is expected to internalize the values of his community. In the nearby Trobriand Islands (where a less unpleasant social life is depicted) this identification is satisfactorily accomplished. Fortune gives us very little direct information about this relationship in Dobu. He says: "One of the most firmly founded facts of the social organization is that the mother's brother constantly gives gifts of wealth and of magic to his sister's son, who inherits all at death" (1963:85). Yet all his explicit information contradicts the picture of solidarity and identity thus drawn; indeed, he gives an explicit contradiction in the next sentence where he points out that the nephew must *extract* from his mother's brother's son the magic which his mother's brother had given to his own child. Let us see what this means, remembering that, in this community of sorcerers, knowledge of sorcery is perhaps a man's most important asset. A man is obliged by law to pass on his magical property to one nephew, but "he usually teaches his child and his sister's child all the magic he knows" (15). And this, as Fortune makes clear, is not only an expression of sentimental affection toward a son but a clear expression of hostility toward his nephew, "a very horrifying and subversive action." That the men thus normally give to their own sons what should rightly be given only to their nephews tells us a great deal about the avuncular bond.

I do not mean to suggest here that a man "naturally" wants ties with his own sons in preference to his sister's—though I believe the proposition well worth exploring—but only that the quality of Dobuan interpersonal relationships derives from the failure to provide *any* kind of identity for the Dobuan child.

To put the matter in terms of our general construct, the society inadequately provides the institutionalized means for the individual to internalize the constraints of society and the constraints upon his own ego-aggrandizing impulses. This is not merely an absence of controls. Controls, in fact, abound; they are in the magical practices of his fellows of which each man is fully aware, and every Dobuan makes at least a public front of controlled behavior and restraint of impulses. Not only are there strict rules of propriety, but also the Dobuan makes every effort to display a face of good behavior (with the result that the missionaries are deceived but the traders are not) and outward signs of conformity and friendliness. (The avoidance of witchcraft talk, of sexual reference, of uncovering one's sexual organs is explicit, while all persons secretly are involved in witchcraft or sorcery and in extramarital sexual activity. Only those too young or too old for sexual affairs are free to use terms of sexual reference.) No, it is neither absence of rules nor the absence of efforts to control others that accounts for the pervasive anarchy on Dobu. It is, I feel certain, the failure to provide internalized restraints on individual impulses through appropriate institutionalization, with the result that these impulses are constantly being enacted for the private purposes of the individual (whenever he can escape detection and direct punishment), who is then suffused with guilt and (by reason of feeling guilty) assumes that others are secretly endeavoring to punish him for these acts.

The lack of internalized constraints, coupled with the sure knowledge that his fellows are similarly unconstrained, the lack of institutionalized discharge of his hostilities against the external constraints to which social life nevertheless subjects him, these aspects of ongoing existence deprive the Dobuan of satisfaction in social relationships. It is little wonder that he tends to engage in incestuous relationships with members of his matrilineal kindred,* not merely because there is a pervasive breakage of rules nor, as

* One gets the impression that mother-son relationships are the only ones with any endurance and warmth and, perhaps by extension, brother-sister relationships. Fortune is clear on the point of fraternal hostility.

Fortune suggests, because the heightened sinfulness of incestuous adultery is provocative and titillating, but because it is the only relationship in which a measure of security can be achieved.

The contrast with the Tallensi—in terms of the quality of organizational means of ordering interpersonal relationships—cannot be questioned. This contrast also demonstrates (though it does not prove) the thesis that the internalized conflict between self-interest and societal demands is the relevant element in the situation, and that the absence of adequate institutionalization, particularly the inadequate "parental" roles, is the essential reason for the pervasive anarchy and hostility of Dobuan society. Considering the variance of Dobuan behavior from that of sister communities in Melanesia, we may assume it is a recent and local growth. I cannot explain why the relative institutional poverty in Dobu has come to be, but would assume that some situational conditions are responsible for exacerbating tendencies which are found throughout the area. However, at this juncture we may disengage ourselves from concern with the historic etiology and concern ourselves only with the character of the disorder and its central elements.

Again we may say that the older culture and personality school would point to child-rearing practices as the significant cause, and here we must say that the patterns of child rearing, as exemplified for instance by early and severe weaning, are consonant with the character of adult hostility. How could it be otherwise, for certainly a population with so little restraint and so little empathy could hardly give to children—however they were fed—the essential elements to build up self images which they can manipulate into meaningful relations to a—as it happens, nonexistent—community.

The dichotomy between self and society which is an internalized dichotomy should, I believe, find some expression in the institutional aspects of culture, either in the structuring of social behavior which we call institutions, or in the metaphysical constructs which we call religion or the system of belief. For this reason I feel that the frequent appearance of dualistic organization of social systems and dualistic emphasis in philosophic systems are both relevant to my thesis.

Philosophical dualism is expressed in many primitive systems of belief as well as being a recurrent feature of the great religious traditions and is at least latent in such modern scientific philosophies as Freudian psychology and "equilibrium theory." I suggest here, without any attempt at proof, that this is a response to the universally internalized conflict. Duality lies in many places in nature: day and night, sunrise and sunset, earth and sky, plants and animals, right and left, etc., and most have been introduced into the symbolic expression of one people or another. But the most insistent, both in its reality implications and its symbolic involvements, is that duality of the sexes with its sociological correlates: the bi-parental character of procreation and hence the basic dual social involvement of every child. Yet tempting as it is to reduce the repetitive dualism in primitive systems to this simple biological fact, I do not think that this adequately comprehends the reality; rather, I think that it is the internal conflict of man which finds social expression in this inevitable and insistent duality in nature. Furthermore, as a consequence of the domestic and hence relatively private role of the women as against the military-juridical (and public) role of the men, the sexes frequently come to symbolize the opposing forces contained in each individual. This, it seems to me, is implicit in the situation described by Evans-Pritchard for the Nuer and reiterated by Leinhardt in his discussion of neighboring Nilotic tribes. The point at least deserves further exploration.

In this section I have sought to lay down a basis for identifying the necessary or relevant functions not only as they relate to the worldly tasks of society, so to speak, but also as they involve the psychological needs of the individual, who is both an independent and a dependent entity, who is both a biophysical object with physiological requirements and a symbolic object with symbolical needs. Though in fact these are intertwined and intermixed in the functioning psyche of the individual, as a practical matter one must examine specific elements of a social order. To do anything else would involve us with not only an exceedingly clumsy but an entirely unworkable model. Thus, as I endeavor to illustrate in succeeding sections what I mean by comparative functionalism, I shall focus on specific postulated social requirements, as, for example, modes of allocating food, the needs and problems inherent in human sexuality, the post-mortem projection of the symbolic self, and the like.

We must not lose sight of the fact that these considerations internal to the social order take place in an environmental context and that, therefore, solutions to social problems are dependent upon matters essentially nonsociological. Food-getting and food-sharing needs will be different in a sparse environment and under technological primitivity from those in a rich environment and with technological advance; control problems will be different in a society endangered by neighbors from those in one in isolation, and so on. I am not here developing a theory of evolution or expounding upon ecology, but I am insisting that both are relevant to the possibilities for and the limitations on social action. Thus the forms which institutions take will not merely be the product of the needs of individuals in society, but will also be situationally relevant.

Finally we must turn to the fact that institutions

beget institutions; that some institutions may be thought of as primary, dealing directly with basic and universal human needs, while others are secondary or tertiary, building upon the needs created by the primary institutions. Thus, for instance, developed political institutions, which are certainly not necessary to human social existence, may be a reasonable and necessary response in areas where large-scale public works, notably irrigation, are a public advantage, or when protection from human predators is necessary. And if institutions of large scale are to remain viable, then perhaps certain additional functions (such as the monopoly on the use of force) become requisite. The essence of my approach to these secondary, derivative, or contingent functional requisites lies in the assumption that they relate, ultimately and through intervening variables, to the essential and primary requirements. This is what is meant by an ecologic analysis. For, to return to the earlier discussion of the context of social life, human requirements are a constant, and cultural differences, if they are to be explained at all, must be explained in terms of adaptation of human needs and capacities to the diverse ecological circumstances under which societies are to exist and which they must exploit with the techniques available to them. Even primary institutional responses to basic social needs are not constant; secondary institutions meeting derivative social needs have a yet wider scope of possibilities. Nevertheless, there is a sufficient degree of functional interrelatedness, a frequent limitation on institutional possibilities, and often a definable advantage to certain solutions over alternative ones in meeting such derivative needs, so that we find within ecological categories that there is often a high degree of similarity in the institutions of social organization. It is this similarity which makes for statistically significant cross-cultural correlations among social phenomena.

V

FUNCTIONAL REQUISITES
AND INSTITUTIONAL RESPONSE

In this chapter I want to demonstrate by example what the comparative functional approach leads to in the way of analysis. I will first take a very basic and essentially simple example with respect to food-sharing, then I will return to the case of the Nayars and the functional implications of sex and parenthood, and third, examine a contingency situation with respect to political systems. After these examples we can return to the broader implications of the approach of comparative functionalism.

Institutions of Sharing

The essential character of human sociality as distinct from group life among other vertebrates (with rare and partial exceptions) is the fact that food-sharing takes place over a wider group than the parents and immature offspring. The institutions for performing this function vary widely, from patterns of mutual generosity to elaborate systems of trade and transport; they vary so widely that anthropologists have despaired of calling them economic institutions (unlike the counterparts in other sectors of human sociality). Yet, if this is a universal function, it is relevant that it be examined as such.

It will be necessary first to pause over the concept of food-sharing (or, more widely, goods-sharing) in order to divest it of some of its secondary semantic connotations. I specifically do not mean to limit it to some kind of communistic, socialistic, or communalistic institution, though such institutions may perform the function; from my standpoint a system of money and markets is as much a goods-sharing institution as are cooperative or communal ones.* By sharing, I don't necessarily mean equitable sharing but merely some pattern of pooling resources and allocating produce. It is again the distinction between the function and the institutional device for performing the function that we must keep in mind.

Now it is precisely my point that the institutions for goods-sharing vary from one culture to another, but that some means of doing so is to be found in all.

* It will be seen that this is a much broader conception of sharing than that of Cohen (1961), who is concerned with the affective aspect of sharing in the sense of giving.

The character of the institutional device will depend to some extent upon the general level and the specific type of production, and upon other aspects of the social order. Furthermore, it may be more efficient in one aspect than in another; that is, one institutional means may be more effective in preventing waste, another in providing for universal rather than partial coverage, and a third in providing incentive for production—and these diverse concomitants may become the central concern of scholars, moralists, or politicians.

For the most part, goods-sharing in industrial and urban societies involves some kind of market system, some means by which tokens are given for work done and exchanged for needs and wants; but, as we well know, most primitive societies do not use this system at all, or at least do not use it for the everyday aspects of life but only for the prestige markers. In the middle range of society there usually exists some kind of corporate group whose membership shares economic resources such as land or fishing places, who may or may not work cooperatively in the labor required for production but who see to it that all members have some minimally adequate share of the necessities for life. We see that in many instances where such societies come under the influence of urban and industrial economic production, these corporate groups continue their economic sharing functions, even though stripped of a good deal of their social and political purposes.*

I want, however, to narrow our focus to the simplest level of hunting and food-gathering, to concern ourselves with what is perhaps the lowest (in the nonpejorative sense of least complicated) social system. For among such peoples as the Andamanese, the Australians, the Eskimo, and the Bushmen, the people are pressed by the limitations of their environment or the lack of technical knowledge, or both, to the very edge of starvation. (This is not true of all hunters and gatherers, for those on the West Coast of North America, from Central California to Central Alaska, had a rich environment and an advanced technology, and they were rich in goods.) These impoverished hunters and gatherers are forced by circumstances to establish some means of sharing, particularly of the large animals killed, for otherwise the successful hunter would not be able to consume his products and in the absence of techniques of preservation the ultimate loss to the community would be devastating. Indeed, it is suspected that in many instances the bands are of such a size that any significant reduction would result in their complete extinction. This suggests that, whatever else is relevant, at this level of cultural development the most important aspect of sharing-institutions is that the coverage be universal

* See, for instance, Kenneth Little (1957), and the broad extension of this phenomenon shown by Ardener (1964).

and minimally adequate to the least recipient, rather than that the emphasis be upon incentive toward production. Be that as it may, we find that universally among such tribes there are mechanisms for the distribution of food. These, as Service (1962) has demonstrated, generally involve a territorially based social unit made up of several separate individual families. These families share the resources but do not necessarily always hunt cooperatively. Yet in every instance I know of there are regulations which provide for sharing the kill among members of the local group. This, as I have already suggested, seems to me to be necessary for survival.

But what is particularly important for our consideration is that the mechanisms for such sharing differ from one community to another. Thus the Andamanese pattern operates through what can best be called institutionalized generosity, where the person who makes the kill has full rights over the animal but where his own social standing depends upon the generosity with which he shares out his booty and the nicety with which he recognizes matters of protocol (Radcliffe-Brown 1964). It relates to the Central Andaman institution of age-deference pattern. The situation is quite different among the Arunta and, I gather, widely so among other Australian aborigines. There sharing in no way depends upon generosity— which, in point of fact, is not a sentiment one feels to be characteristic of these people—but upon the specific obligations of kinship. Among the polar Eskimo, on the other hand, the natural environment provides deep-freeze preservation and the obligations of sharing are less insistent. However, any cache may be freely used by a person in need, which provides functionally (but in an institutionally quite different manner) the essentials of food-sharing at this cultural level, i.e., the minimization of starvation.

We need not go further; I think the point is clear. Though food-sharing functions are universal and have certain specific characteristic elements in common at the lowest levels of cultural development, they are nevertheless institutionally quite diverse. And the broader point is that because the sharing function is performed by diverse institutions—even at the same level of culture—the character of this universality is obscured by an institutional approach to the problem while it is illuminated by a functional comparison.*

Functional Restraints in Sexuality and Procreation: A Reexamination of the Nayar

In chapter II I spent some time examining Nayar marriage in order to demonstrate the inadequacy of

* Sahlins' (1965) essay has just come to hand; it treats the recurrence of sharing functions. Sahlins is concerned with taxonomy and definitions, but an examination of his cases offers ample evidence for the diversity of institutional forms and the continuity of functional relevance.

the best reasoning (within the tradition of the comparative institutional approach) in performing the essential task of anthropology, and to raise the epistemological problems inherent in reified concepts. I now want to return to the Nayar in order to apply the functional approach, which I believe makes sense out of the data which the institutional approach serves to obscure. My purpose, of course, is to demonstrate the nature and validity of my approach rather than to shed light on the Nayar.

Since we do not start with institutions but rather with functions, we must develop out of our theoretical presuppositions those functions which generally revolve around what anthropologists intuitively call marriage. Since, incidentally, this also includes the family (as procreating and nurturing unit) we cannot entirely escape a concern with the group normally constituted as a result of marriage.

I want to direct attention to the following functions:

1. Delineation of rights to sexual access, including the public presentation of those rights and the sanctions against breach.

2. Provision for the nurture of infants and the care of pregnant and lactating mothers, including the definition of rights and obligations, and publication through the community of the existence of such a collaborative group and the delineation of its personnel.

3. Provision of a defined social status and social identity for the child.

4. Provision of education and indoctrination of the child, and particularly the presentation of adult models for behavior for children of both sexes.

5. Provision of an identification object for both parents through which they may project themselves into the future through sociologically established descendants.

Let us not concern ourselves either with whether this is a complete list of functions or with their further justification. It would be possible to be more explicit; one could say, with respect to the delineation of sexual rights, for instance, that this further requires ideological support in the sense that some rationale must be involved or, for the provision of infant care, the rights and obligations of the parties to the collaborative action must be defined in detail to assure performance and avoid conflict. But again I avoid these involvements in order not to impede the program of analysis.

In most cultures, there is some ritualized act involving a man and a woman which performs all of these functions (and performs them publicly). This we call marriage, in analogy to marriage in our society, but there is no self-evident reason that they must all be packaged together in one institutionalized act. Ethnographic fact indicates that they are not universally so packaged, as the Nayar case indicates, but it is perhaps more surprising that they usually are so packaged.

What, if any, institutions among the Nayar perform these functions? There is first the *tali*-rite, the ritual of "marriage" of a prepubescent girl, in the absence of which she may not legitimately have intercourse or bring a child into the society. The "husband" is drawn from lineages standing in a defined relationship. This rite fulfills the first function; it makes sexually accessible to each woman certain classes of males and, contrariwise, of course makes her accessible to them. It defines this explicitly in the sense that she may have intercourse with certain classes of men and not others, but loosely in the sense that she may have many liaisons operating at a time, and of whatever duration is mutually desired. This high level of sexual freedom is unusual and we are not surprised to learn (assuming that this is a potentially disruptive factor) that there are many subsidiary arrangements defining and delimiting the kinds of social intercourse men and women may have when they are engaged in a sexual liaison. Except for a very ancillary involvement with the fourth item, this rite does not serve any of the other functions listed.

The second ritual act which forms part of what Dr. Gough has included in Nayar marriage is the ritual acknowledgment by one or more males currently engaged in sexual liaisons with a woman that they are the "father" of her child, when she has become pregnant; this ritual being the payment of the midwife's very nominal fee. This institution is manifestly concerned with our third item, but again it does so only in the sense of reaffirming the legitimacy of the child; that is, if the ritual act takes place, the child may have a social identity; if not, it is killed or ostracized along with its mother: the ritual does nothing to provide the specific identity for the child.

It will be interesting to see, however, what this second ritual actually does. Quite clearly it serves as a policing mechanism on the mother against breaches of conduct with respect to sexual involvements. Though Nayar women are free to make liaisons widely, they are not absolutely free in this. The Nayars are a group of subcastes in a highly caste-oriented society and, aside from what may be called incest rules, the only sexual restriction is that a woman may have intercourse only with men of her own station and above. The ritual of acknowledging paternity must of course be performed by such a man; it follows that through refusal to acknowledge paternity the men can bring the most stringent sanctions possible against a woman who engaged in sexual misconduct, as the Nayar define it.

Nayar "marriage," as Gough uses the term, serves only to delimit the choice of sexual partners and give legitimate status to offspring. It does not define the status of the child (except to recognize its social existence), which is done through the lineage of the mother, nor does it create a nurturing institution, which exists as an ongoing corporate group in the form of the matrilineage.

Before taking up the fourth listed function, I would like to make some comment about the fifth. I have suggested that there is a tendency for persons to want to project themselves into future generations, a kind of wish for eternal existence. This is more ordinarily statisfied among women, whose role in procreation is more explicit and involved; in men the matter requires social definition. At least such a function is frequently performed, whether it is requisite, psychologically useful, or a secondary feature of some more fundamental institution. Nayar marriage does not provide this opportunity for men. Though a man claims paternity (singly or with others), his claim does not create an enduring social bond with the child and thus does not serve such a psychological function. The man who pays the midwife fee is called by a kinship term by the child only as long as he maintains the sexual liaison with the mother, and all her other sexual partners are called by the same term. Gough elsewhere makes it clear that though the Nayar recognize the role of genitor, a man has "no right to interfere in any way in his child's training," and quotes the adage that "no Nayar knows his father" * (Gough 1962:364). Nor does a man project himself with satisfaction onto his sister's son, for there "the etiquette of behavior between a man and his mother's brother was formalized to the point of avoidance" (348–349), even though the latter was responsible for the youth's training; and it is not surprising to learn that there regularly was "deep hostility in their interpersonal relationships." However, let us return to the character of the relation of men to their sexual partners and their offspring. Gough writes (1959:172):

This does not mean that men did not sometimes form strong emotional attachments to particular wives † and their children. My information indicates that they did. I know for example that if a man showed particular fondness for a wife, his wife's matrilineal kin were likely to suspect the husband's matrilineal kin of hiring sorcerers against them. For the husband's matrilineal kin would be likely to fear that the husband might secretly convey to his wife gifts and cash which belonged rightfully to his matrilineal kin. This suspicion was especially rife if

---

* Gough also says that "a man is said to have been especially fond of a child whom he knew with reasonable certainty was his own. He would make small gifts to him, play with him on visits, and offer him friendly counsel as he grew older" (1962:364). This suggests a pervasive and disruptive conflict between the human wants and the institutionally demanded deprivations.

† Gough uses the terms "husband" and "wife" for sexual partners in regular liaison.

the husband was a *kāranavan* who controlled extensive property.

This passage contains, it seems to me, a most important message. As I read it, it asserts that despite institutional pressures against doing so, there is a recurrent tendency (one would like to have a measure of frequency) for men to seek permanent psychological ties with both their sexual partners and their children, and that such ties are viewed as threats against the established order so that institutionalized means must be provided to prevent, through severe sanctions, this disruption from occurring.

The Nayar of the Haripad area in Travancore offer evidence for the pressures that I believe inhere in the situation described by Gough. In a recent paper she writes:

I was told by several people that during the early nineteenth century, most Nayar round Haripad became cultivators rather than soldiers, and that the more prosperous "middle-class" Nayar gradually shifted toward residence in avunculocal extended families, priding themselves on their ability to maintain the wives and children of their male members as well as, when necessary, to uphold their old obligations to the women and children of the matrilineage. Gradually, indeed, it came to be thought shameful for men to "creep in" to the *taravads* of their wives. This statement, too, is confirmed by Panikkar for the Nayar of Central and South Travancore generally (Gough 1965).

The first point to be made is that these facts show that the Nayar do not provide a negative case with respect to masculine desire to identify with offspring, despite the *institutional* fact that they do not do so. That is, it does not, in itself, provide disproof of the universality of the fifth functional element listed above. (It does not, of course, prove it to be true either; no single case could. One might fairly assert the alternative hypothesis that these men were compelled to adopt such antisocial sentiments by the prohibition itself.) We are too prone to take such negative examples of near-universal behavior as disproof of universal tendencies without examining the actual pattern of action that the institutional situations have evoked.*

We are not told why the Nayar, in contrast to other people with lineage systems, should find sexual liaisons so potentially disruptive, and I must return to this point, which is of greatest significance for my thesis. But before doing so, I must examine the situation with regard to the fourth postulated func-

---

* Let me reiterate this point through a linguistic analogy. Hockett points out that the presumed linguistic universal, the distinction between nouns and verbs in all languages, was denied by Nootka. "But it turns out [he writes] that even in Nootka something very much like noun-verb contrast appears at the level of whole inflected words. Therefore, although Nootka forces the abandonment of the generalization in one form, it may still be retained" (Hockett 1963:3-4).

tional element: the creation of a masculine bond, of an identification for the child.

The essential peculiarity of the Nayar system is that it fails to create a close and enduring interpersonal relationship for a man either with a sexual partner or with a child. From the child's point of view—particularly the male child—there appears to be no person who relates to him in the role generally assigned to a sociological father, except the very arid role of household head in the matrilineage. However, I am impressed with the functional implications of the *absence* of such paternal ties. In order to appreciate this, let me first emphasize that the Nayars are a part-culture in a plural society; that they are the soldiery in a militaristic society; and, further, that the maintanance of the military machinery has importance in the wider social arena in which the Nayars served as soldiery. I quote again from Gough (1959: 177):

Marriage and paternity were probably significant factors in political integration. For hypergamous unions bound together the higher sub-castes of the political and religious hierarchies. Multiple sexual ties, as well as the *enangar* relationship, linked office-bearing lineages to each other and to their retainers in a complicated manner. And Nayar men phrased their loyalty to higher ranking military leaders, rulers, and Brahmans in terms of a debt owed to benevolent paternal figures whose forebears had collectively fathered them and whose blood they were proud to share. The generalized concept of fatherhood thus commanded the Nayar soldier's allegiance to his wider caste unit, to the rulers of his village, chiefdom, and kingdom and to his religious authorities. It was associated with tender loyalty and with fortitude in war.

Now the ritual father of the *tali*-rite and (so long as he maintains the sexual liaison) the pater who paid the delivery fees to the midwife are both called by a father-term which has the meaning of lord in the caste-hierarchical sense. We see a translation, a cultural identification, and an institutional reinforcement of paternity orientation to the militarized caste —all expressed in the idiom of kinship terminology. We see that the functions usually performed as part of the marriage institution are now performed by the caste-military institutional system. Indeed, we learn that the child is inducted into military training at the age of seven, while young adults (fathers) are away from their villages a good part of each year, engaged in military service. We find evidence that the function of identification is thus re-formed, and it is fruitful to inquire why it is thus.

First, I should point out why the more usual pattern is not requisite; why, so to speak, it is *possible* for the lineage to do without fathers. This possibility exists because the Nayar are a part-culture in a plural society. Though the Nayar are farmers, lower castes do the daily masculine chores on the land; the Nayar are utilizing the labor of others to free themselves from the requirements of performing the usual nurturing roles. (And it is not without interest that it is these farm hands who are prevented, through the sanction of the midwife fee payment, from making free with their economic mistresses.)

Though this circumstance makes it *possible* to redirect the father orientation, it does not tell us the positive functions such redirection performs. Yet, it seems to me, there are positive reasons for such redirection, in terms of the national life of which the Nayar are a part. The masculine identifications certainly create an orientation to the military system and give psychological reinforcement to the hierarchical scheme of the caste society and to the pattern of loyalty of soldiers for their commandants. It is calculated to make of them ideal soldiers, unfettered by those economic, social, and psychological ties to home and hearth which are the bane of generals in most citizens' armies. Yet institutionally the Nayar reproduce themselves and have adequate outlets for their sexuality without the nuisance of prostitutes or camp followers. From the standpoint of functional relevance, the disengagement of young adult men from their ties to any domestic ménage and the redirection of personal identification of youths from their paters and genitors to the military-caste hierarchy both make eminently good sense.*

* I find that subsequent to this analysis, Gough herself recognizes the functional relevance of the peculiar marital

At the same time, the disengagement of males from their domestic ties with their own matrilineages must make these latter more vulnerable to the potentially disruptive effects of sexual involvements—a question raised earlier in this section. Hence the strict prohibition against sexual liaisons between the women and their domestic underlings; hence, also, the protection against the encroachment of other alien males upon the social citadel, the matrilineage. And above all there is the restriction (which Gough cites as part of her justification for calling this a marital system) against two persons of the same economic unit having sexual access to the same partner (as quoted above, p. 20). This rule suggests to me that the Nayar were fully aware * of the explosive potentials of their own sexual freedom.

I would like, in closing this discussion of the Nayars, to point out that the questions I have addressed to the Nayar case through the emphasis upon function are different from those asked when one starts with the institutional assumption; that, in fact, they cannot be asked from this latter point of view.

---

customs in Central Kerala Nayar. She writes: "These arrangements appear to have been consistent with Nayar men's traditional occupation as soldiers, and with the fact that the matrilineally owned estates were cultivated by tenants and serfs" (Gough 1965).

* I do not really mean to anthropomorphize the emergence of customs in this way; the Nayar may not have been so aware but merely may have, in times past, been discomfited by these potentials.

Thus something can be learned about the functional character of Nayar life, about the interrelationship of institutions, and about the secondary and unanticipated consequences of existing institutions that would have been overlooked without this approach. These are the kinds of functional questions that tend to be asked by those scholars who engage in functional analyses of individual societies on the Malinowskian model but which become obscured in the comparative analysis or institutional treatment. To engage in this exercise is not in itself something new. The internal analysis of social systems done from a sophisticated viewpoint often "explains" the peculiarities of local custom.

But in the comparative functional approach we are not interested in explaining Nayar idiosyncrasies; we are concerned with an understanding of social phenomena. What is important to our analysis, therefore, is the relation of Nayar behavior to that of other systems of behavior. More specifically, we are concerned with what the Nayar case does to our generalization about functional requisites of a social system and problems inherent in community life. For, I repeat, we have been prone in anthropology to quote the negative case as disproof of generalizations about man, while its function should be to refine the character of these generalizations.

After examining the Nayar case can it be said with certainty that men do not everywhere seek to project themselves into the future through their own paternal (or avuncular) role? Or that male children do not require a masculine role model? Or that a masculine role model creates a pattern of loyalties and social direction in the child? Or that free sexuality implicit in the Nayar case does not create potentials for disruption through masculine jealousy and that therefore institutions for the control of such sentiments are not requisite? These are the kinds of elements which I believe to be appropriate to any model of society. The Nayar case cannot prove their validity; this we know. But the tendency to use the Nayar case and other unusual patterns to disprove generalizations has dominated social theorizing, and particularly such generalizations as those in the questions just asked. Insistence on terminological purity and the comparison of institutions cannot resolve these problems; the examination of functional requisites makes such resolution possible. But we cannot continue to rest our case on the examination of specific individual cultures; we must endeavor to discover that which is universal, either to all known societies or to all societies operating within some clearly established limitations. That is, we must turn to comparative functionalism.

Contingent Functions: Statecraft

Another sector in the organization of social behavior that has evoked much fruitless terminological discourse has to do with the systems of control; that is, with political or governmental institutions. Efforts to define the state, to define feudalism, and similar subjects have brought us but a very short distance in understanding this aspect of social life, since they have all failed for the very reason set forth here. I have discussed this problem elsewhere (Goldschmidt 1962), at a time when the idea of comparative functionalism was less well formulated in my mind, and much of what I say now goes over the same ground but with some difference in approach. I want to give this matter some attention here because it enables me to exemplify the problem of contingent functional elements. Food-sharing and orderly sexual arrangements, lying as they do in the central biologically oriented aspect of human behavior, can be seen as universal elements in social life; but statecraft may be considered a secondary institution which, if it is to be viable and effective, has its own requisite elements. But before examining political institutions as such, I must make some more general remarks about the character of human controls. My thesis that society mediates between the self-oriented impulses of the individual and the needs of social collaboration places this phenomenon as much within the basic framework of biological man as are food-sharing and sexuality. Thus my first point is that one must distinguish between the functions of governance and the institution of government; the former are universal, the latter limited.

Strictly speaking, whenever one person in a society

has the explicit or implicit right to order the behavior and actions of another, as a part of an established role, there is an act of governance. No society can operate without such role definitions. These roles may, and generally do, exist within the family, clan, corporation, or any other institution.* Control of individual behavior by other personnel operates within every general type of institution—household, kin group, religious cult, economic unit, or whatever types the particular society may develop, such as associations, age-sets, etc.—and generally all of these institutions, collaboratively or in opposition to one another, serve the functions of governance.

Any effort to define a state and to make a hard and fast distinction between states and acephalous societies is bound to run into difficulties. Yet some societies have developed special institutions to perform the governmental roles, either entirely separate from all others or warping existing kinship, religious, or economic institutions to the purpose of maintaining order over a large territorially integrated population. When this happens we speak of the people as having a state. Because statecraft is concerned with control and the ultimate weapon of control is the use of physical force, the existence of statehood is often defined in terms of the monopoly on the use of force

* This problem was clearly recognized by such students of political institutions as MacIver (1947) and Lowie (1927).

(carefully laying aside the fact that the psychological powers of a priestcraft or the economic powers of owners may have more effect than the sanctions of legitimate physical coercion). In short, there is no single criterion to distinguish states from nonstates, and there are many intermediate and poorly realized systems in the ethnographic record which have some elements of statehood.

Let us pause a moment over societies clearly characterized by the absence of developed political institutions—societies of hunters and food-gatherers and of true agriculturalists of the kind labeled acephalous in the anthropological literature (Fortes and Evans-Pritchard 1940). Many such societies are organized into small independent bands; so small as to render contrary to commonsense meanings the use of the term states, even though they may have a loose council of elders who do, in point of fact, render and enforce public decisions binding upon the community. These bands are independent but not separate from sister-bands with which alliances and marriages are regularly made.

At a somewhat more advanced level of society—what is often referred to as the "middle range of societies"—territorialities are found that consist of a number of separate but mutually interdependent familistic units occupying an area. These units (defined in terms of filiation and descent and using the sentiments of kinship to maintain their internal order) are not normally subordinated to a system of superordinate authority, but arrive at over-all governance through the adjudication of disputes, operating on shared notions of propriety and a recognition of their mutual need and interdependence. The Tlingit offer an excellent type case where the matrilineal house groups, clans, and moieties operate as a hierarchy of separate corporate groups, but there are innumerable cases in the literature of ethnography. If the lines of organization are well developed and the cultural values strongly reinforced, as was clearly the case on the northwest coast of North America, this can be an effective means of maintaining internal harmony, and even for protection against and exploitation of neighboring peoples. Elsewhere, as among the Hupa and Yurok of Northern California, where the organizational devices were less effective, there was no means of mounting an integrated, large-scale offensive against neighbors or even of collaborative protective action—a condition well attested to in the literature —and we may assume that only the character of the terrain and the absence of stronger political forces enabled that system to remain viable.

That familistic organization of the corporate kin group kind can be extremely effective is demonstrated by the League of the Iroquois. Fundamentally, the League represented a single simple institutional innovation, and one that can by no means adequately place it in the ranks of true statehood as that term is generally defined. This innovation was a provision for the maintenance of internal harmony within the member tribes and clans so that none would at any time endanger the others, and the further provision that none would engage in any military action that did not have the sanction (though not necessarily the cooperation) of all. Beyond this, the League, despite its resounding titles and elegant organization, had no political or administrative functions, yet this was enough—at that particular time and place—to enable the Iroquois tribes to be a scourge throughout northeastern North America, and effectively to exploit the surrounding peoples.* Until Europeans began to develop powerful communities, there was no more effective organization of peoples in the area.

But the essence of statecraft, that is, of institutions which provide for the orderly internal control of a large population, however much it is dependent upon the right to control its constituent population, does not lie in the phenomenon of control as such. The real question that must be asked of state-organized society is: What is accomplished as a result of such

* I do not want to imply that all that is involved in such activities is in the organizational devices as such. The effectiveness of the Hupa-Yurok organization lay in the value placed on self-denial and hard work; the power of the Iroquois was in great measure dependent upon their values of fortitude and courage, and even their carefully fostered cruelty.

institutions that is not possible—or is extremely tenuous or difficult—in their absence? From the evolutionary view, the establishment of effective political controls makes possible a broader base for sharing, accumulation of greater amounts of capital, development of larger public works, greater protection against outside dangers, and greater ability to exploit outsiders. All of these accruals give political institutions a positive valence, when the technological apparatus is sufficiently advanced to make it feasible and fruitful to organize into large units, and when the environment of other societies makes it advantageous to exploit them or to protect oneself from them.

But we must remember that every political order not only has control-over-people as the essential ingredient of its existence, it also involves the internal struggle over who shall be the incumbents in its system of control, for clearly the very existence of a political system feeds the opportunity for individuals to further their personal gain, in terms both of creature comforts and the status of their symbolic selves. It is this distinction to which M. G. Smith (1956) alludes when he separates administrative from political systems. Thus from the standpoint of the maintenance of the system we must consider not only what is relevant for the society as a whole, but also what is serviceable to the preservation of the status of the elite. Where there are irrigation works or other large-scale enterprises, where there is the threat of external expropriation (or appears to be), or where the system itself succeeds in exploiting neighbors, there is adequate payoff to the rank and file, and system maintenance reduces itself as a problem. It is no accident that the strong states known to ethnology —notably the Baganda, the Inca, the Aztec—were profitably engaged in such exploitation and that this profit was widely distributed in the form of rewards to a large corps of the citizenry. Similarly, the strong states of history have repeatedly if not universally been associated with irrigation as a central economic instrument, where the rewards of central controls are manifest to every peasant, however much he is subjected to abuse and exploitation (Wittfogel 1957, especially chap. 3).

Now these considerations are necessary to explain the origin of states, or the transformation of apolitical into political societies,* but are not necessary for the understanding of the continuation of political institutions, nor for conquest and subordination, for in the latter cases there exists a sector of the community which has a strong vested interest in its own maintenance and which is in a position to preserve, or try to preserve, the system which serves it so well. Thus we

---

* In Africa societies appear to have crossed back and forth over the border between nonpolitical and state systems with some frequency (or to have had, in varying degree from time to time, the functional elements of statecraft). The Shambala are a case in point (Winans 1962).

can set aside, for our problem of functional relevance, the whole matter of whether political institutions are themselves necessary and turn to the question: If political institutions do exist, what, if anything, are the requisite functional elements?

We may speak of a fully developed state as existing when the role of authority, placed in the hands of a person or group, extends over the personnel of a territory, involves substantial elements of their life activity, and when the group is so large that authority must regularly be transmitted through intermediaries. From the functional point of view it is then possible to ask: What are the functional requirements for the fulfillment of such a system, over and beyond those requisite for all social systems? I suggest the following:

1) The establishment of roles defining the rights and obligations of the authority center.
   a) The transmission of these roles to new incumbents.
   b) Sanctions supporting these roles.
   c) Symbolic representation of these roles.
2) The articulation system between the authority center and the personnel.
   a) The location of lines of communication between the center and peripheries.
   b) The sanctions for intermediate role positions.

   c) The containment of these intermediaries so as to prevent usurpation of power.

3) The provision of conflict resolution mechanisms.

   a) Among citizens or constituent groups.

   b) Between such citizens or groups and the center of authority.

4) The provision of protection against external threats to the structure.

5) Economic support of the authority system itself, and of its personnel.

The point is not that we have taken a familiar list of governmental functions as we know them (executive, administrative, courts, military, taxation) and rendered them into other language, but that we have listed functions as such—functions which not only may be variously performed but are performed in very different ways in different societies.

Thus the power role may be defined by a formally drafted constitution, by an evolving set of customs embodied in a few recorded acts, by religious ideology, or by an elaborated historical myth. These may be legitimized by appeals to natural right, divine right, biological superiority, or historic mission. Power itself may be transmitted by inheritance (variously patterned), election, court revolution, or an interregnum of anarchy and the brute use of force among contenders. The system may be articulated on a geographic base, a syndicalist base, direct clientship, or through the idiom of kinship. We need not go on. Our task is merely to show that structural differences do not constitute a basis for delineation, that the essence of statecraft lies in the performance of a specific set of functions through whatever institutional device is available, so to speak, for the purpose.

But we must remember that contingent functions are not requisite in an absolute sense, and thus may not be requisite at all. Are there, in fact, politically organized, centrally controlled, extensive communities of a kind which common sense compels us to call states, yet which lack one or more of these postulated functions? I think there are—that instances are to be found in Africa, where a great variety of politically organized societies have come into being. If this is the case, is there any possible test of the relevance of the postulated items? I think there is. We can ask two questions of the data on inadequately realized political systems: what are the conditions under which they are viable? and, what consequences can be observed which appear to result from the failure in the performance of certain functions? I would expect, as answer to the first question, that inadequately realized political institutions are operative where no strong external threat to the society is to be found or where these institutions are nevertheless the most powerful unit in the community of societies of which they are a part. The Iroquois offer a case in point. I might also look for nonpolitical strengthening devices, such as the harnessing of religious zeal to the purposes of internal control; that is, a heightened sense of social cohesion or social mission through a strengthened ideological support.

But more important is the consequence, and here is where history and social anthropology should collaborate. For not only are political institutions notably volatile, not only are dynasties (incumbents in the role of controlling institutions of statecraft) repeatedly overthrown, but states as organizations also come and go. A military leader, like the Zulu Shaka, can create a quick empire, but its institutional arrangements are inadequate to survive the temporary results of a religious zeal and an opportunity for exploitation. The history of Africa appears to be full of examples of states of limited duration, just as is Europe's prior to the development of major industrial enterprise (which gives value to stable large-scale unities). The question is, of course, whether the recurrent demise of political systems can be seen as institutional failure, and through this kind of inquiry to determine whether the functional elements of statecraft listed above are, in fact, requisite to viable political organization.

VI

CONCLUSIONS

Although a distinction between contingent and immediate functional requirements has been formulated in the previous chapter, in one sense all functions are contingent. They are contingent upon survival, not of each and every person in the community, but of the society as such. It is a debatable proposition whether without institutions it is possible for man to survive; it is self-evident that his numbers would be greatly altered if all institutional devices were removed. But this is not merely to make the tautological observation that if the institutions were different then the society would be different: it is to make the much more important statement that if necessary functions (whether contingent or not) are not performed the society will decline in strength, consumption of goods, and ultimately in population; that is, that survival is dependent upon such functions as are necessary being, in fact, performed. The conditions of life vary in time and space, and what is needed under harsh physical conditions may not be required under more lax circumstances; what is needed if a people is pressed by enemies may be unnecessary under conditions of isolation; what is needed for a large and diverse community will not work in a small and homogeneous one. We are impressed with the degree to which the human animal can function with many of his organs removed, and under favorable conditions function unimpaired. This does not mean that the organ in question serves no function (though manifestly it may not, as apparently is the case with the vermiform appendix), but only that it can be circumvented; it means that the function is not necessarily (i.e., always and inexorably) necessary. I think the analogy is apt: that not every institution in every society performs a function, that many of the functions can be elided without disaster or even major disruption to the body politic. At least I would entertain this as a possibility. I believe, however, that some functions are requisite and that the failure to provide them would have disastrous effects on the community.

An institution may be more or less efficacious in performing a particular function; that is, if institutions are instrumentalities, some may be (in a given situation) more efficient tools than others. This also has self-evident appropriate biological analogies. Here we may note, too, that not every problem has a perfect or satisfactory solution. The dilemmas that inhere in social systems frequently find expression in institutional adjustments; these dilemmas may either be compromised or satisfy one element by aggravating another. A society with limited total resources (as frequently found among peasants) may either pass on property to one son, leaving the remainder disenfranchised, or by equal distribution threaten the economy of each; it may, with sociologically explosive potentials, endeavor to compromise by making sons joint entrepreneurs. None of these institutionalized means of handling inheritance can avoid the difficulties that are the result of the variation in the number of children and the proportion of the sexes from one family to another. This leads us to another generalization about functional requisites. Institutions often —and perhaps always—have unintended consequences; the solution of one problem may raise others which, in turn, require solutions and receive similarly imperfect ones. A stock-keeping people requires not only physical care of the animals but protection against predators, especially human predators. Such people must be trained to fight and indoctrinated in the values of military effectiveness. But this indoctrination, necessary for the preservation of herds, becomes an incentive for aggressive raids that can escalate into warfare, and this in turn requires both the elaboration of military operations and the institutions for arrival at a resolution. Chain reactions are not limited to inert matter.

Returning to the matter of contingency, this—as a

moment's reflection will show—is the essential assumption in all ecologic studies of social behavior. That is, the ecologic thesis builds a corpus of expectations based upon a certain environment and a means of its exploitation. The unspoken assumption is that the people are utilizing the environment to the best of their ability in terms of technological resources available, and are adjusting their institutional patterns to the needs these economic forces create. To take an example that has engaged my attention recently (Goldschmidt 1964), the demands of large livestock in arid, nonindustrialized lands place certain burdens upon the men and tend to create certain basic similarities in the structuring of interpersonal behavior. The fact that the empirical data on pastoral social structure reveal a high level of consistency—a high correlation of crude observations—supports such a hypothesis. But my point here is merely to recognize that the ecological hypothesis itself is one that asserts: if a people is to engage in large-animal pastoralism under semiarid conditions, then certain functional elements are contingently requisite.*

* E. R. Leach has discovered the important consequences of the ecological factor in peasant life. He writes: ". . . if we repudiate the Durkheimian emphasis on moral rules and jural obligation then the problem becomes much simpler. The constraint imposed on the individual is merely one of patterning and limitation; the individual can do what he likes as long as he stays inside the group. For purely technical reasons, connected with the pro-

CONCLUSIONS

Now the essence of this ecologic approach is not that the same conditions create the same institution; it is, rather, that similar conditions bring forth comparable problems, and similar problems evoke similar solutions. We end up by formulations which say that, for example, agnatic segmentary systems are highly correlated with nomadic pastoralism, but we are no longer concerned with whether these are the same in

---

cedures and efficiency of irrigated rice agriculture, the arrangements of the Pul Eliya ground are difficult to alter. They are not immutable, but it is much simpler for the human beings to adapt themselves to the layout of the territory than to adapt the territory to the private whims of individual human beings.

"Thus, . . . Pul Eliya is a society in which locality and not descent forms the basis of corporate grouping; it is a very simple and perhaps almost obvious finding, yet it seems to me to have very important implications for anthropological theory and method" (1961a:300–301).

It is indeed an obvious finding, one that most modern American scholars would have taken as a basic assumption. However, the difficulty with which Leach arrives at the solution makes the accomplishment all the more impressive; and the difficulty derives, as Leach explains a page or so further on, from the fact that ecological considerations are *presumed* to be taken into account by such social anthropological classics as Evans-Pritchard's *The Nuer*, but in fact *never do* actually enter into the explanatory analysis. The same is true of Daryll Forde's early textbook. On the other hand, Emrys Peters (1964) demonstrates a perfect use of micro-ecological adaptation in his analysis of the relation between structuring of kinship behavior and the pattern of rainfall in North Africa.

all particulars or are highly divergent. We are divested of all concern with the semantic unity, and hence with the epistemological implications of our institutional terms. There is a good deal of evidence that a high correlation exists between agnatic segmentary kin unities and nomadic pastoral economies.* I believe that such an organizational system is eminently suited to the purpose, utilizing the universally applicable sentiments of filiation, making the males the central element in a system requiring masculine physical characteristics both for the major economic activities and for the prevalence of military action, and establishing a system of articulation which enables a swift change from individual decision-making to large cohesive centrally controlled entities. But from the standpoint of their ecological considerations it may make no difference whatsoever if these entities are sometimes endogamous, as indeed the ethnographic literature suggests. Since, however, marital rules are so closely tied in the anthropologists' minds with the functionally central elements of kin units, we find it difficult to disengage ourselves from the importance of these marital regulations. We bring ourselves only with difficulty to call both endogamous and exogamous filiation units by the same term. Or, rather, we do so only when we divest ourselves of the

* The generic point is made by Sahlins (1961) but I do not agree that predatory invasions of territory is the significant independent variable.

notion that the word somehow stands for an existential entity (as is implicit in Gough's use of the term "marriage").

At the same time, segmentary lineages are not the only viable means of satisfying the requirements of pastoralism. Age-sets can perform some of the same functions—especially those associated with the military—with equal effectiveness, as the data on the Nilo-Hamites of Africa and the emergence of military societies on the plains of North America attest.

It should be noted in passing that this approach to functionalism, together with the processes of ecological adaptation, forms the basis of a modern evolutionary approach to culture history. Indeed, it requires only the notion of accumulation of technological knowledge through time, and the assumption (already made) that a society adapts preexisting patterns to new situations, to establish the basis for an evolutionary system. This is the underlying assumption of the recent book by Elman Service,* in which he seeks to show certain social unities within broad categories of technological level. It is also the underlying assumption of Julian Steward's major thesis (Steward 1955), as well as of my own discourse on the topic (Goldschmidt 1959). But in all these instances the

* But in this Service (1962) is leaving his Whitean predilection and we note the significance of his dedication of the volume to Julian H. Steward along with Leslie White.

results are marred by too great a concern with institutional unities and insufficient concern with functional relevance—a circumstance admittedly difficult to overcome in the face of the character of ethnographic reporting.

At the outset of this essay I suggested that the central idea of comparative functionalism has been implicit in a good deal of anthropological writing over the past decade or so. While it is neither possible nor pertinent to make a complete survey of such tendencies, it does seem worth while to indicate some of the evidence that this is the case, and in so doing give recognition to some of the sources out of which the conception grows. I have already cited Huxley's (1955) quest for a "comparative physiology" of culture, and noted that Almond (1960), with a similar aim in mind, has been influential in developing comparative political analyses, and appears to be seeking a formulation within which an appreciation of functional unities can be achieved without regard to institutional diversity. The linguists (who so frequently serve as a model for cultural anthropological approaches) have turned to a search for universal elements in language,* and this, it seems to me, inevitably involves a kind of comparative functional-

* See Greenberg (1963, *passim*), especially Charles F. Hockett, "The Problem of Universals in Language," and Joseph H. Greenberg, "Some Universals of Grammar with Particular Reference to the Order of Meaningful Elements" (Greenberg, ed. 1963). The problem is also dealt with in a posthumous paper by Kluckhohn (1961).

ism in this realm of culture. As already indicated, the newer evolutionists also express views that carry implications for the position being developed here.

More particularly, there is an implicit orientation in the direction of the comparative functional approach among those anthropologists who have a psychological orientation to cultural phenomena, though this has not, so far as I am aware, taken any explicit formulation. The work of Whiting and Child (1953) and the numerous cross-cultural comparisons that have developed from that effort subsequently, and the more recent controlled comparison of child-rearing practices in six cultures (B. Whiting, ed., 1963; Minturn and Lambert, eds., 1964) are all efforts to examine social responses to postulated universal needs under diverse circumstances. The same may be said of much of the work of Yehudi Cohen (1961, 1964). Both Whiting and Cohen recognize the importance of ecology as the significant variable for understanding the diverse social responses to fundamental human needs.

I believe, also, there is developing an interest along the lines suggested in this essay, among the social anthropologists themselves. I have already noted Leinhardt's dissatisfaction with classic functional explanations. It seems to me Fortes' examination of the relevance of the Oedipus and Job myths to African societies is pertinent, and a recent presentation by Peters (also already cited) is suggestive. Thus it may very well be that even among those who have stood for a Durkheimian point of view, who have denied universal human needs and endeavored to study social structure without regard to the human constituents, are beginning to alter their stance. In this light, it is perhaps worth while to digress a moment over the implications of the work of Floyd G. Lounsbury. Kinship studies have a special place in anthropology; they have been of particular importance to the structural school of functionalists, who find in them an opportunity to relate one aspect of social behavior— the system of classifying kin—to others, especially formation of corporate groups and the regulation of marriage. In doing so, the role of the individual and the universality of human needs have both been either ignored or denied. Lounsbury has developed an algebra for analyzing kinship terms and finds that the essential elements of any system can be reduced to a few basic rules—the precise nature differing with each system, but the general character remaining the same. The results of his careful analyses and the logic of his method lead Lounsbury "to the assumption that the *primary* function of kinship terminologies is to delineate the relation of ego [i.e., the speaker] to the members of his personal bilateral kindred in such a way as to express some socially and legally important aspect of each of the relationships" (Lounsbury 1964:382). To those outside the controversies in the realm of kinship this might seem to be a statement of the obvious, but as Lounsbury makes quite clear, it represents a radical departure from doctrine. It is radical because it assumes a generic functional role, concerned with individual needs and human characteristics.

Again, the work of Leach, though still within the framework of structural anthropology, shows an effort to divest itself of the limitations inherent in classic functionalism. This is indicated not only by his approach to the family (Leach 1955) and his acceptance of ecologic forces already cited (Leach 1961a), but more particularly in a later essay, "Rethinking Anthropology" (1961b). His effort to divest himself of institutional terminology is an indication of a changing orientation; by adopting a topological approach, in which internal relationships between institutional elements are more important to the understanding than are the institutions themselves, he seeks to remove the epistemological problem that has engaged our attention here.*

* The antipsychological stance of many British scholars suggests, however, an unwillingness to go as far with the use of psychological assumptions as the approach of comparative functionalism demands. Thus Leach exhorts us not to "drag in private psychological theories behind a smoke screen of technical terms." Of course it can be shown that he nevertheless does so, as when he writes, "Now it seems to me arguable that a sibling link is '*intrinsically*' more durable than a marriage tie" (1961b:120,

CONCLUSIONS

But the difficulties inherent in a true functional approach remain as a major deterrent to proper cross-cultural analysis of social behavior. We slip so easily from a start at functional analysis into a delineation of entities and a concern with taxonomies. Thus I was hopeful as I began a recent paper by George Dalton (1965) that the subject of money might be treated functionally,* but in the end I got only a taxonomy, a distinction between commercial and primitive money-stuff, and (having been offered only a discourse on an ancient product by an amateur anthropologist) merely learned what all of us already know, that primitive (subsistence) societies do not frequently use such goods for ordinary daily transactions.† What Dalton does not provide is a discussion of such functions of the wealth symbols that are occasionally called money as: the need to spread risk, the accumulation of capital, the requirement for markers in a system of exchanges

---

his quotation marks but my emphasis). Or again when he discusses, in his reprinted article "Cronus and Chronus" (1961b: 125), the intrinsic aspects of time as they influence human thought.

* Dalton opens his essay with a concern over the application of Western concepts to primitive societies, and the function money plays there.

† The Hupa and Yurok of northwest California did, but only in times of emergency. It is the only instance in a pre-agricultural society that I know. *See* my "Ethics and the Structure of Society" (1951).

(whether for economic goods, prestige goods, or wives), the use of wealth symbols as instrumentalities for deflecting a direct confrontation, and the like.*

As I said at the outset, the functional approach here being advertised makes for a new and difficult view of cultural behavior. We are trapped by our linguistic habits into the use of reified terms applied cross-culturally (and it is no better to apply a term from one primitive society to another than to apply one

---

* Spreading risks both over population and through time is perhaps the most important and obvious function of prestige goods. This can be done directly, as with the accumulation of livestock and the widespread pattern of livestock exchange transactions. But it can be done symbolically under primitive conditions, as when a Blackfoot Indian purchases with many horses a "medicine bundle," which (while the society was operative) is readily reconverted into other assets. All prestations have this kind of function, however much we want to sentimentalize gift-giving in primitive communities. The classic case is in the Northwest Coast potlatch where, as Helen Codere (1951) so cogently has demonstrated, the goods are not only given as a matter of creating obligations, but are used as a means of battle with other groups—battles often for the control of resources. And a moment's reflection should make us aware that, in the absence of a judicial system, availability of wealth items becomes all but essential as a functional element to deflect retaliation and further bloodshed through the payment of wergild. Or to put it differently, how can a society lacking third-party decision apparatus adequately handle the resolution of conflict if there is no "wealth" with which the guilty party can buy off the act of murder?

from our own society), and we endeavor to resolve these problems by refinement in definition and the elaboration of taxonomies. The resolution lies in the search for commonality of functions.

The thesis of this essay may be briefly summarized as follows:

1) Because each culture defines its own institutions there is always an element of falsification when we engage in institutional comparisons among distinct cultures, and

2) Because no causal analysis can be demonstrated with single cases, no matter how clearly developed or intellectually satisfying they may be,

3) Therefore, it is necessary to engage in the comparison of the performance of functions to determine:
   a) Whether they are universally performed, and
   b) If not, then whether there are any special circumstances or any special consequences of failure of performance.

4) Functions, however, are derived from a model of social organization, a model developed out of existing experience with societies.

5) The groundwork for such a model was developed, which recognizes:
   a) That human societies always operate within a field, constituted of the psychological

character of man, the character of the physical and social environments within which it is in operation, and the heritage of knowledge and techniques available to it; and

b) That the organization of society mediates between these factors.

6) The functions performed in a society are essentially of two kinds:

a) The work-jobs requisite to the fulfillment of the biologically based needs (and their cultural derivatives) of the population for survival, and

b) The organizational devices necessary for the preservation of collaborative action demanded by these work-jobs.

7) This latter function involves the essential conflict, internalized in the individual, between self-interest and community interest, which means that the normal individual must be adequately supplied with an appropriate self-image to function as a member of society, while at the same time his energies are harnessed for the functions of collaborative behavior.

8) While some functions relate to universal human characteristics, others are contingent upon circumstances or situations in which there may be an element of choice, but it is possible to develop a set of contingent functional requirements for defined situations.

The burden of the program as set forth is to provoke a new approach to the oldest problems of the anthropological enterprise. We have moved away from the questions which our discipline was designed to answer, and for which answers we alone have access to certain crucial data. Anthropologists have adequately demonstrated that man lives in society (as social anthropologists contend) and according to customary procedures (as cultural anthropologists contend), and most of our sister social scientists have come to accept the force of each of these parameters —even sometimes, I fear, to give them too much attention. But the essential questions remain: What is the nature of man? What are the limits of his adaptability to situation and his malleability to cultural demands? For surely we can no longer pretend to believe that he is *any*thing, can *be* anything, or *may* be anything, under *any* circumstances. What, therefore, are the recurrent problems of human interactions? What are the tenable solutions to these problems? What are the secondary consequences to such solutions?

While it is true that no human can ever be truly culturally innocent, it is still not true to say that human behavior is culturally determined. While it may be true that it is possible, out of cultural motives, to make *some* individuals do almost anything and many individuals do *some* things, it is not true that culture can make *all* persons do *any*thing. What is even more germane is that when peoples are constrained by cultural forces to act in certain ways—say to remain celibate—not only are particular institutional devices required to attain such ends but the process entails certain consequences for the individual. Melford Spiro has pointed out that psychological involvements may be seen as intervening variables in the functional relationship between two sociological elements; similarly, from the standpoint of individual psychology, the sociocultural element may be seen as the intervening variable in the functional whole of the human personality.

It is no longer adequate to deny the reality of postulated human characteristics with the simple statement: But it isn't so in Pago Pago. Yet the classic institutional approach leaves us helpless to this familiar retort. Some years ago I wrote an essay in which I pointed out that people are more alike than cultures; that social demands are normative, while the average behavior under any culture tends toward the center of the range for humans as a whole (Goldschmidt 1956). There is, I suggested there, a good deal of evidence that, for instance, the average Zuñi and average Kwakiutl man behave a good deal more like each other than the normative patterns of the two cultures are alike. The suggestion is pertinent to a recognition of the limits and potentialities of man, to the behavior he is prone to. It is not merely an expression of the limitations of culture as a process involving human adaptiveness; it is suggestive of the nature of man to which culture must adapt.

Many generalizations about the nature of man have been summarily dismissed because some cultural studies have lightly given them the coup de grace on the basis of a few exceptional cases, without adequately examining the character of these exceptions. Let me, in concluding this essay, set forth a few of these generalizations which I feel should, at the very least, be treated less cavalierly.

1) The natural element of sexual jealousy. Have our studies really demonstrated that with both males and females there is not normally a strong feeling involved with respect to sexual partners that desires exclusive access, and that the acquisition of secondary spouses or lovers does not serve basically as a threat, a feeling of deprivation, or some such sentiment? And, what is the sentiment? When closely examined, are the instances of sexual freedom really satisfactory to both parties?

2) Contrariwise, do not the members of both sexes regularly or repeatedly want access for themselves to additional sexual partners? And, as a corollary, is the relative frequency of polygyny and of double standards favoring masculine freedom merely an expression of male dominance or does it express some difference

in masculine sexuality—perhaps only effective in middle or late years of life after the woman has borne a succession of children?

3) If sharing-institutions (as defined earlier) are truly universal, does this mean that man is (as Prince Kropotkin and Ashley Montagu have suggested) fundamentally a loving creature, or is it a necessary institutional device to preserve society against the essential self-interest of the human individual? Is the distinction between mine and thine a universal one for those goods and services which have scarcity or symbolic meaning, or both, and are these everywhere caught up in the symbolic representation of the human self? Is the repetitive arrangement of a careful quid pro quo in the acquisition of wives to be seen as an expression of this social phenomenon, or are there cases (currently not in the central attention of anthropologists) where women are not treated as ego-gratifying chattel which must be carefully husbanded; and, if so, under what circumstances or with what consequences is this diversity associated?

4) Do men everywhere seek some kind of symbolic eternity, and what are the alternatives available for such a search: religious belief, good works, descendants? Is this related to the apparent universal desire for children despite

the manifest hardships entailed in childbirth (or contrariwise, is the "desire for children" merely a repetitive social device for preserving the human community by counteracting natural indifference)?

5) Is war inevitable? Does the absence of military conflict among such tribes as Pygmy and Eskimo have any bearing upon the matter whatsoever, inasmuch as war (as usually defined in an institutional approach) is situationally impossible and unrewarding among such people, though fighting (at least among the latter) is a frequent occurrence? This question does not turn on finding a proper definition of war, but on examining the functional involvements of organized conflict—involvements in the economic sphere, in the organization of society, and in the psyches of the personnel. For warfare is not only widespread, it is an important means of galvanizing a community, an element in preservation of a sense of solidarity and in individual validation of personal status. And it is in these terms only that we can seek the resolution of the pressures toward military conflict. For this purpose, the characteristics of a peasant population of a nation (which may itself be warlike) may tell us more about the consequences of peaceableness than the Eskimo.

CONCLUSIONS

Finally, we must divest ourselves of the implications of cultural relativism. Certainly it was necessary for anthropology to go through a relativistic phase in order to relieve social philosophers of the habit of evaluating cultures in terms of our own culturally determined predilections. Yet by now we can certainly appreciate the contextual value of infanticide without advocating it, or can see the merits and demerits of polygyny without concern over our own convictions or regulations. What we must do now is examine the consequences of particular institutional devices for the stability of the community and the physical and mental health of its constituent members. There are enough instances on record of primitive peoples not being happy in their own customs but (like many a married couple) not knowing how to escape them, such as the case of the Ajamaroe (described by Barnett 1959), so that we, too, should begin to understand the phenomenon of dysfunction and establish relevant criteria for functional efficacy. This means, among other things, that we anthropologists must rid ourselves of the Rousseauean "good savage," must cease to use ethnographic data either as an escape or as a vehicle for expressing our personal social discontent, and begin to look at primitive societies for what they can tell us not only about the possible but about the probable, and about the consequences—to individuals and to societies—of either.

Only the anthropologists (or other scholars adopting the anthropological knowledge and approach) can answer such questions empirically. We have a responsibility not to fritter away our quickly dwindling heritage with irrelevancies, which means that we must build on theory that recognizes the multidimensional character of the human scene or must test models of behavior that are forged in other disciplines —but which only anthropologists can adequately test because of our monopolistic position with respect to cross-cultural data.

It is for this reason that a call for a comparative functionalism is not only necessary but long overdue. In this call I have not specified the elements of a model for testing—which is beyond the scope of any one person today—but have set forth a schema for developing more specific models by indicating both the parameters of the problem and the kinds of questions which the comparative functional approach can, I believe, give answers to. Comparative functionalism contains, I think, the seeds of a new view of culture itself.

REFERENCES CITED

Aberle, David F.
   1961 Matrilineal descent in cross cultural perspective. In: *Matrilineal kinship*. David M. Schneider and E. Kathleen Gough, eds. Berkeley and Los Angeles, University of California Press.

Aberle, D. F., A. K. Cohen, A. K. Davis, M. L. Levy, Jr., and F. K. Sutton
   1950 The functional prerequisites of society. Ethics 60:100–111.

Almond, Gabriel
   1960 Introduction. In: *The politics of developing areas*. Gabriel Almond and James Coleman, eds. Princeton, University Press.

Ardener, Shirley
   1964 The comparative study of rotating credit associations. Journal of the Royal Anthropological Institute, Vol. 94, Part 2, 201–229.

Baerends, G. P.
   1958 Comparative methods and the concept of homology in the study of behaviour. Archives Neerlandses de Zoologie, Vol. XIII (Supplement), 401–417.

Barnett, H. G.
   1959 Peace and progress in New Guinea. American Anthropologist 61:1013–1019.

REFERENCES CITED

Benedict, Ruth
  1934 *Patterns of culture*. Boston, Houghton-Mifflin.
Boas, Franz
  1962 *Anthropology and modern life*. New York, W. W.
         Norton & Company, Inc. (First published 1928.)
Bohannan, Paul and George Dalton, eds.
  1962 *Markets in Africa*. Evanston, Northwestern University Press.
Caudill, William A.
  1962 Anthropology and psychoanalysis, some theoretical issues. In: *Anthropology and human behavior*.
         A. F. C. Wallace, ed. Washington, D.C., The Anthropological Society of Washington.
Codere, Helen
  1951 *Fighting with property*. New York, J. J. Augustin.
Cohen, Yehudi A.
  1961 Food and its vicissitudes: a cross-cultural study of sharing and non sharing. In: *Social structure and personality: a casebook*. Yehudi A. Cohen, ed.
         New York, Holt, Rinehart and Winston. (First published 1955.)
  1964 The establishment of identity in a social nexus: the special case of initiation ceremonies and their relation to value and legal systems. American Anthropologist 66:529–552.
Dalton, George
  1965 Primitive money. American Anthropologist 67:44–65.
Erikson, Erik H.
  1963 *Childhood and society*. 2nd edition. New York, W. W. Norton & Company, Inc.
  1965 Ontogeny of ritualization in man. Symposium on ritualization and behavior in man. London (MS).
Evans-Pritchard, E. E.
  1951 *Kinship and marriage among the Nuer*. London, Oxford University Press.

Firth, Raymond
  1951 Review of: *The web of kinship among the Tallensi,* by Meyer Fortes. Africa 21:157.

Forde, Daryll, ed.
  1954 *African worlds.* London, Oxford University Press.

Fortes, Meyer
  1959 *Oedipus and Job in West African religion.* Cambridge, The University Press.

Fortes, Meyer and E. E. Evans-Pritchard, eds.
  1940 *African political systems.* London, Oxford University Press.

Fortune, R. F.
  1963 *Sorcerers of Dobu: the social anthropology of the Dobu Islanders of the western Pacific.* E. P. Dutton Paperback edition. (First published 1932.)

Frake, Charles O.
  1962 The ethnographic study of cognitive systems. In: *Anthropology and human behavior.* A. F. C. Wallace, ed. Washington, D.C., The Anthropological Society of Washington.

Gluckman, Max
  1959 *Custom and conflict in Africa.* Glencoe, Illinois, The Free Press.
  1963 *Order and rebellion in tribal Africa.* London, Cohen and West.
  1965 *Politics, law and ritual in tribal society.* Chicago, Aldine Publishing Co.

Goldschmidt, Walter
  1951 Ethics and the structure of society: an ethnological contribution to the sociology of knowledge. American Anthropologist 53:506–524.
  1953 Values and the field of comparative sociology. American Sociological Review 18:287–293.
  1956 Culture and behavior. Proceedings of the International Congress of Ethnological and Anthropological Sciences, Philadelphia.
  1959 *Man's way, a preface to the understanding of hu-*

man society. New York, Holt, Rinehart and Winston.

1962 Foreword. In: *Shambala, the constitution of a traditional state*, by E. V. Winans. Berkeley and Los Angeles, University of California Press.

1964 Pastoral society as an ecologic adaptation in sub-Saharan Africa. Wenner-Gren Symposium on Pastoral Nomadism, Burg Wartenstein (photolithographed).

Gough, E. Kathleen

1959 The Nayars and the definition of marriage. Journal of the Royal Anthropological Institute 89:23–34, and reprinted in *Cultural and social anthropology*, Peter B. Hammond, ed., 1964, New York, Macmillan Co.

1962 Nayar: Central Kerala. In: *Matrilineal kinship*. David M. Schneider and E. Kathleen Gough, eds. Berkeley and Los Angeles, University of California Press.

1965 A note on Nayar marriage. Man 2.

Greenberg, Joseph H.

1963 Some universals of grammar with particular reference to the order of meaningful elements. In: *Universals in language*, Joseph H. Greenberg, ed. Cambridge, M. I. T. Press.

Hempel, Carl G.

1959 The logic of functional analysis. In: *Symposium on sociological theory*, Llewellyn Gross, ed. Evanston, Row, Peterson.

Hockett, Charles F.

1963 The problem of universals in language. In: *Universals of language*, Joseph H. Greenberg, ed. Cambridge, M. I. T. Press.

Hooker, Evelyn

1965 An empirical study of some relations between sexual patterns and gender identity in male homo-

REFERENCES CITED

REFERENCES CITED

sexuals. In: *Sex research, new developments*. John Money, ed. New York, Holt, Rinehart and Winston, Inc.

Huxley, Julian
  1955 Evolution, cultural and biological. In: *Yearbook of Anthropology*. New York, Wenner-Gren Foundation.

Jarvie, I. C.
  1965 Limits of functionalism and alternatives to it in anthropology. In: *Functionalism in Social Science*. Don Martindale, ed. Philadelphia, American Academy of Political and Social Science.

Kaplan, David
  1965 The superorganic: science or metaphysic. American Anthropologist 67:958–976.

Kluckhohn, Clyde
  1944 Navaho witchcraft. Cambridge, Papers of the Peabody Museum of American Archaeology and Ethnology, Vol. 22, No. 2.
  1961 Notes on some anthropological aspects of communication. American Anthropologist 63:895–910.

Kroeber, A. L. and Clyde Kluckhohn
  1963 *Culture, a critical review of concepts and definitions*. New York, Vintage Books, Random House. (First published in 1952.)

Leach, E. R.
  1955 Polyandry, inheritance and the definition of marriage: with particular reference to Sinhalese customary law. Man 55, and reprinted in Leach, E. R., 1961, *Rethinking anthropology*, London School of Economics, Monographs on Social Anthropology, No. 22.
  1961a *Pul Eliya, a village in Ceylon: a study of land tenure and kinship*. Cambridge, The University Press.
  1961b Rethinking anthropology. In: *Rethinking anthropology*, London School of Economics, Monographs on Social Anthropology, No. 22.

145

REFERENCES CITED

Lounsbury, Floyd G.
  1964 A formal account of the Crow- and Omaha-type
        kinship terminologies. In: *Explorations in cultural
        anthropology: essays in honor of George Peter
        Murdock*. Ward H. Goodenough, ed. New York,
        McGraw-Hill.
Leinhardt, Godfrey
  1964 On the concept of objectivity in social anthropol-
        ogy. Journal of the Royal Anthropological In-
        stitute 94:7.
Lévi-Strauss, Claude
  1962 *Totemism*. Translated from the French by Rodney
        Needham. Boston, Beacon Press.
Lewis, Oscar
  1955 Comparisons in cultural anthropology. In: *Cur-
        rent anthropology*. William L. Thomas, Jr., ed.
        Chicago, University of Chicago Press.
Little, Kenneth
  1957 The role of voluntary associations in west African
        urbanization. American Anthropologist 59:579–
        596.
Lowie, Robert H.
  1927 *The origin of the state*. New York, Harcourt
        Brace and Co.
MacIver, Robert W.
  1947 *The web of government*. New York, Macmillan
        Co.
Martindale, Don, ed.
  1965 *Functionalism in social science; the strength and
        limits of functionalism in anthropology, eco-
        nomics, political science, and sociology*. American
        Academy of Political and Social Science, Mono-
        graph 5, Philadelphia.
Merton, Robert K.
  1948 The self-fulfilling prophecy. Antioch Review,
        Summer issue.

Minturn, Leigh and William W. Lambert, eds.
1964 *Mothers of Six Cultures: Antecedents of Child Rearing.* New York and London. John Wiley and Sons.

Nadel, S. F.
1952 Witchcraft in four African societies: an essay in comparison. American Anthropologist 54:18–29.

Nagel, Ernest
1961 *The structure of science: problems in the logic of scientific explanation.* New York, Harcourt, Brace & World.

Oliver, Symmes C.
1961 Ecology and cultural continuity as contributing factors in the social organization of the Plains Indian. University of California Publications in American Archaeology and Ethnology, Vol. 48. Berkeley and Los Angeles, University of California Press.

Peters, Emrys L.
1964 Camel herding pastoralism and linear organization in Cyrenaica. Wenner-Gren Symposium on Pastoral Nomadism, Burg Wartenstein (photolithographed).

Radcliffe-Brown, A. R.
1964 *The Andaman Islanders.* New York, The Free Press of Glencoe. (First published 1922.)

Radcliffe-Brown, A. R. and Daryll Forde, eds.
1950 *African systems of kinship and marriage.* London, Oxford University Press.

Rieff, Philip
1959 *Freud, the mind of the moralist.* New York, Viking Press.

Royal Anthropological Institute
1951 *Notes and queries in anthropology.* 6th edition. London, Routledge and Kegan Paul.

Sahlins, Marshall D.
1961 The Segmentary lineage; an organization of pred-

atory expansion. American Anthropologist 63: 322–345.

1965 On the sociology of primitive exchange. The relevance of models for social anthropology. A.S.A. Monographs, Tavistock Publications, London.

Schneider, David M. and E. Kathleen Gough, eds.

1962 *Matrilineal kinship*. Berkeley and Los Angeles, University of California Press.

Secoy, Frank

1953 Changing military patterns on the Great Plains. Monographs of the American Ethnological Society, Vol. 21, New York.

Service, Elman R.

1962 *Primitive social organization: an evolutionary perspective*. New York, Random House.

Smith, M. G.

1956 On segmentary lineage systems. Journal of the Royal Anthropological Institute 86:39–80.

Steward, Julian

1955 *Theory of culture change: the methodology of multilinear evolution*. Urbana, University of Illinois Press.

Tolstoy, L.

1949 *The Cossacks*. New York, Pantheon.

Wallace, Anthony F. C.

1962 The new culture-and-personality. In: *Anthropology and human behavior*. A. F. C. Wallace, ed. Washington, D.C., The Anthropological Society of Washington.

Whiting, Beatrice B. ed.

1963 *Six Cultures: Studies of Child Reading*. New York, John Wiley and Sons.

Whiting, J. W. M. and I. L. Child

1953 *Child Training and Personality*. New Haven, Yale University Press.

REFERENCES CITED

Winans, E. V.

    1962 *Shambala, the constitution of a traditional state.* Berkeley and Los Angeles, University of California Press.

    1965 The political context of economic adaptation in the southern highlands of Tanganyika. American Anthropologist 67:435–441.

Wittfogel, Karl A.

    1957 *Oriental despotism: a comparative sudy of total power.* New Haven, Yale University Press.